THE SPIRITUAL JOURNEY OF

JOHN WESLEY

A Study of his Doctrine of Christian Perfection

Stuart J. Burgess

To

Elisabeth with love

Acknowledgements

I wish to express my thanks to those who have assisted me in this study, and especially:

The Revd. A.R. George, M.A., B.D. President of the Methodist Conference 1975-76, and recently holder of the Lamplough Chair of Biblical Studies and Liturgy at Wesley College, Bristol; The Revd. Professor John Heywood Thomas, B.A., D.D., S.T.M., Professor of Theology at the University of Nottingham and to Susan Kinchin who typed the script.

Foreward

The Christian is called to be on a spiritual journey which takes us beyond time to eternity. Our origins lie in the desert and we are called to be a pilgrim people. Although we belong to a community of the Easter People we often travel alone and it is through individual journeys that we can all benefit.

The Methodist People and the larger Church owe a debt to John Wesley whose life spanned almost the whole of the 18th Century.

In May 1988 the Methodist Church celebrated the 250th Anniversary of the 'heart warming' experience and the liturgy used at St. Paul's Cathedral, London, is included in the Appendix.

This study of John Wesley's spiritual journey is but a small contribution to celebrate that occasion.

TABLE OF CONTENTS

1

INTRODUCTION

No one would deny Wesley's pre-eminence as preacher, organiser and Church leader, and few can be found who will dispute his right to be called 'holy'. Piette writes of Wesley:

> "he has been compared to St. Benedict as regards his liturgical sense and piety: to St. Dominic for his apostolic zeal: to St. Francis of Assisi for his love of Christ and detachment from the world: To St. Ignatius Loyola for his genius as an organiser"[1]

Overton describes Wesley's life as

> "the busiest and in some respects, the most important life in that century".[2]

Yet it is when we turn from Wesley as an evangelist, organiser and Church leader, to Wesley as philosopher and theologian that opinions differ concerning his intellectual contribution to the theology of the Church. No one would claim that his chief contribution to his generation or subsequent ones was an intellectual one. The natural bent of his mind was practical rather than speculative. Wesley had no other concern that to "save souls" and he would have taken only the slightest interest in the opinion of subsequent generations of his status as an "intellectual". He did not share William Law's scorn of scholarship but in a letter to the author of "The Serious Call" he stresses the danger of mixing philosophy and religion. He reminds Law of his own earlier opinion on the point:

---

1. M. Piette "John Wesley In the evolution of Protestantism", p. 480.
2. Overton "John Wesley" Preface v.

> "Religion is the most plain, single thing in the
> world. It is only 'We love Him, because He
> first loved us'. So far as you add philosophy
> to religion, just so far you spoil it".[1]

In the preface to his one hundred and forty-one sermons, he says plainly:

> "I abstain from all nice and philosophical
> speculations, from all perplexed and intricate
> reasonings; and as far as possible, from even
> the show of learning".[2]

Wesley did not desire to offer anything new in doctrine. He believed that everything he taught was in the New Testament and in the authorative documents of the Church of England. If what he preached appeared new he would show that it was in the Scriptures. His "Notes on the New Testament", which have been a standard of Methodist doctrine for a century and a half, were largely borrowed. Vulliamy in his book "John Wesley" says

> "We cannot give John Wesley a place among
> the great intellectual reformers of the
> Church".[3]

Eayrs[4] and Piette[5] conclude that Wesley was no great thinker either as a philosopher or theologian. He might have been but he saw his life in different terms - that of telling people in plain

1. Works IX p. 466.
2. Works V ii
3. Vulliamy "John Wesley" p. 359.
4. Eayrs "Wesley - Christian Philosopher and Church Founder", p. 107.
5. Piette "John Wesley in the evolution of Protestantism", p. 435.

words the things which belong to their sanctification. The
principal stress of his teaching falls not on opinions and doctrines
but on a way of life.

Yet this should not lead us to overlook the importance of the
theoretical foundation of Wesley's message which unites a
strongly didactic with a prophetic element. Several of his
publications are devoted exclusively to the treatment of problems
of central importance in theology. By making everything turn on
Christian experience Wesley was able to pass beyond the proofs of
the truth of religion advanced by such contemporary philosophers
as Berkeley and Butler.

The general structure of Wesley's Christianity has usually
been described as a theology of experience. His affirmation of
Christian experience is considered his main characteristic. Wesley
and the Evangelical movement in England were seen as
reactionary phenomena - an emotional reaction against an earlier
intellectualism. The reaction marks a transition from natural to
supernatural religion. Wesley emphasised the necessity of God's
self-revelation, although through the presence of the Holy Spirit a
person is able to enter into immediate communion with God. Cell
maintains that Wesley reacted against humanism, Arminianism
and went "Clean over to a theocentric doctrine of Christian
experience".[1] Bett claims that Wesley founded a religion and
theological in the fact of experience[2]. Experience, if it is genuine,
must agree with Scripture but experience is regarded as the final

1. Cell, "The Rediscovery of John Wesley", p. 5ff.
2. Bett, "The Spirit of Methodism", p. 129f.

authority. It is in this that Bett sees the main contribution of Methodism to modern theology thought and method. It was, of course, from this appeal to experience that Wesley's doctrine of perfection sprang. Wesley's belief in God's universal will of salvation was based upon his appeal to experience. There is a danger in over-stressing the appeal to experience. Lee points out that in Wesley inward, individual experience is subject to the control of the Bible, particularly as interpreted by the early Fathers. Lee says that the typical thing about Wesley is his "contribution to mystical experience with the ethical, the rational, and the institutional elements in religion".[1] Wesley himself was fully alive to the danger of making too much of individual experience - if man is not to go astray it must be checked by the Bible.

Yet, the fact remains that Christian experience played a most important role in Wesley's theology. Scripture was the obvious foundation of it to which he always referred but it was interpreted in the light of experience.

> "I have endeavoured to describe the true, the scriptural experimental religion, so as to omit nothing which is a real part thereof, and to add nothing thereto which is not".[2]

This experience was not simply his own personal experience but that of the Christian fellowship and he constantly corrected his understanding and interpretation of the truth by comparison with that given to others.

---

1. Cell, "The Rediscovery of John Wesley", p. 321f.
2. Sermons I, p. 32 (preface).

Much attention has been given to Wesley's idea of justification and sanctification. This book aims to consider Christian perfection within the general scheme of spiritual progress as suggested by Wesley. Sanctification is rarely presented in its full range. The concept is normally restricted. Sometimes it means Christian perfection only, no regard being made to the gradual development of sanctification from its commencement in the New Birth. Sometimes entire sanctification is minimised. Sanctification must be seen in its full scope and in its due relation to the concept of salvation as a whole.

CHAPTER ONE
THE EIGHTEENTH CENTURY SETTING

Wesley was essentially a practical person and the doctrine which is to be considered was for Wesley of practical importance to the people. A study of a person's doctrine - especially where emphasis is laid upon experience - must be seen against the background of the times. England in the 18th century was a land of contrasts. On the one hand the reading public was growing. The great writers of Queen Anne's day - Addison, Swift, Defoe, - still flourished in the reign of her successors, and their works achieved popularity. Defoe's "Robinson Crusoe" which appeared in 1719 is one of the greatest works of fiction in the English language. The 18th century saw the publication of such novels as "Pamela" (1740) written by Samuel Richardson which took the form of letters supposed to be written by a servant girl. Sir Christoper Wren died in 1773 and the Renaissance architecture which he had done so much to popularise was the favourite style in England for another 100 years. Handel came to England in 1710 and helped to introduce the Italian opera to London. After this he turned to Oratorio and the 'Messiah' was first performed in Dublin in 1742. Bath in the 18th century was a town under the reign of Beau Nash, king fashion, who ruled supreme in the Pump Room and the Assembly Room. The tune of the stately gavotte filled the ballroom, the white-wigged dancers moved sedately to their places, as the candles shone on the dresses - the gay silks and satin of men and women.

On the other side of the coin there was a large section of the
people who were living in conditions of social hardship, danger
and discomfort. The Cornish tinners, among whom Wesley
preached for 50 years, worked under-ground with hardly any
room to turn their bodies. A doctor who worked among the
miners saw his patient conveyed to a hut full of naked children
and destitute of all conveniences and many necessities. The moral
condition of these people was as deplorable as their physical state.
Drunkenness was common in every village. Brutal sports, such as
cock-fighting and bear baiting, were usual. This too was the hey-
day of smuggling. England at the beginning of the 18th century
was still chiefly a land of villages - there were no large towns
except London and agriculture was the occupation of the vast
majority of people. Next in importance to agriculture came
spinning and cloth making and that too was carried on in the
country where the people made the woollen cloth in their own
cottages. Two tremendous changes took place in the 18th century
which altered England. The first was the enclosure of the common
fields which was accompanied by a revolution in the methods of
farming. Jethro Tull (1710) invented a machine for sowing seed.
The second was the coming of machines or the industrial
revolution. The first inventions were applied to the old woollen
industry and to the manufacture of cotton. It was within these
new centres of population that Wesley won his greatest victories,
where the established church was helpless in the changing
conditions. The enthusiasm and fire of the new movement were
suited to the violent social and economic upheaval that was
proceeding. Miners and labourers, factory workers and slum
dwellers were uplifted by a faith which enabled them to ignore

their earthly miseries. Only a small percentage of the people could read and writing was a luxury. Superstition flourished and fortune-tellers had a large public. Belief in ghosts and evil spirits was general. When popular education stood at such a low level it is obvious that this would necessarily be reflected in the pattern of popular amusement. It was unspeakably coarse. Particularly popular were the hangings at Tyburn jail, then sought after as free entertainment. The youth at the time used to go about in crowds and attack peaceful passers-by, preferably women, throw them into holes, or put them in barrels and roll them down a hill. To break a nose, knock out a few teeth or an eye was not uncommon. It was also common practice to give people a 'sweat-cure'. This consisted of a number of young people standing round the victim with drawn swords, pricking him so that he was kept continuously in motion. It might be an act of revenge or simply 'pure' pleasure. Gambling was also popular. The politician, Charles James Fox, lost two thousand pounds playing cards in one evening. Obviously only a very few could play for such sums but even so it would not be wrong to call gambling a national disease. It is clear that such crude pleasures could only flourish upon liberal recourse to alcohol. In 1684 gin was introduced into England. Women with small children drank as heavily as the men. There was also permissiveness in the sexual sphere. The theatres presented plays that were immoral. Nor was respect for human life very great. A hundred and sixty different types of crime were punishable by death and many were the victims of these inhuman laws. At the close of the seventeenth century a society was formed for the reformation of morals. This society had houses of ill-fame in London closed down wholesale and was responsible for bringing a number of law breakers to be called to account. Some gamblers, drunkards, offenders against the Sabbath, and swearers were either fined or imprisoned or flogged by the public executioner. In this way a number of obvious abuses were brought under control but society did not have the power to introduce real change. These contrasts became less sharp as the century advanced because some of the slums gave place to more spacious residences and some of the prevalent vices were brought under control and Methodism had a far-reaching effect on the habits and morals of the population. Yet much of this social progress was nullified by the growing effects of industrialisation in the last third of the century. The increasing demand for industrial labour herded masses of people into insanitary towns without reasonable accommodation, provision for health, leisure or education or any distinction between the working capacity of men, women and little children.

It was the business of the Church of England to minister to the spiritual and moral needs and to a lesser extent to the intellectual and social needs of the people of England during this century. The excusable, but not very devout, practice of attending Holy communion in the Parish Church just often enough to qualify for national or municipal office was stopped by the Occasional Conformity Act of 1711. The Whigs resisted the measure but the Tories forced it through. Deprived by their beliefs of a university education, the Dissenters set up academies to train young men for the ministry and other professions. The Tories could not stomach this possible intrusion of Dissenting intelligence into Anglican preserves and passed the Schism Act to dissolve every Dissenting place of learning but as Queen Anne died at this point the Act was never put into operation. The Church of England was exhausted and impoverished by the conflicts of the preceding century. The Puritans had left or been driven from the ranks of the Established Church. The Non-Jurors, who included in their ranks several men who could have given great leadership to the Church as a whole had gone. Rarely can a national Church have been so lacking in leadership and cohesion for so long a time. The chief cause of chaos was the failure of the Houses of Convocation to meet for any useful purposes. It is true that the Convocation had done nothing for many years (since 1664) but when it was revived in 1700 it had some chance of resolving the acute Clerical dissensions of the time. The chance was lost in uninterrupted wrangling and recrimination between bishops and clergy. Rupert Davies says,

> 'It might have been a disaster if they had
> continued to meet. It was certainly a disaster
> that they did not meet.' [1]

The result was that each bishop was left to do what was right in his own eyes in his own diocese. Confirmations, if they took place at all, were of vast numbers of people at once and some bishops were so exhausted by the long ceremony that they resorted to the bestowal of a general blessing. Some bishops scarcely thought it worth while to visit their dioceses at all. Yet, in spite of all this there were some good bishops. Gilbert Burnet, whose origins were in the Church of Scotland, was Bishop of Salisbury from 1689-1715. His theology leaned to the side of broad rather than strict orthodoxy but his administration and pastoral care of his diocese

---

[1]. R. Davies: Methodism, 1963, Penguin.

were beyond reproach. So far as the parish clergy were concerned there were many incumbents and curates who applied themselves diligently to the care of souls. But even in the well-run parishes it was rare for the Eucharist to be celebrated more than once a quarter - unless the parson was a Methodist - and there was often only one service on a Sunday. A single clergyman could hold several livings at the same time. Certain members of the clergy never appeared at all in some of their parishes though they were careful to collect their dues. The appointed a stipendary curate on a starvation wage and let him look after the work as best he could.

There was also contrast in the intellectual and spiritual atmosphere. The so-called Cambridge Platonists, notably Benjamin took the heat out of theological controversy. They stood for reasonable religion and urged that the highest form of Christianity consisted in a mystical approach to God which in its later stages transcended reason and led the soul up to the knowledge of the Idea of the Good. It was their insistence on the power of reason that most influenced their pupils - the Latitudinarians, who became almost the dominant school in Anglican Theology for the first part of the eighteenth century. Where revelation conflicted with reason, revelation must give way. Those who held this view have come to be called Deists but many Latitudinarions did not believe very differently. John Locke (1632 -1709) claimed to be a sound Christian. He professed to find in the Bible a simple natural religion on which all men of sense could agree. John Tolond's 'christianity not mysterious' (1696) inaugurated the cult of Deism. These attacks on Christianity were not left unanswered. George Berkeley turned his attention to one of his principal concerns - natural theology. The result appeared in 1732 under the title of Alciphron, or The Minute Philosopher, and is a general defence of the Christian orthodox position. More famous is Butler's Analogy of the Christian Religion (1736) which admits that Christian truths are not demonstrable but only probable and asserts that probability is the guide of life. William Law, the non-juror, also entered the lists against the Deists. In his Case of Reason (1732) he holds that God gives the knowledge of Himself directly, through the feelings and through mystical apprehension, so that reason is not really necessary for the purpose. These are only three of the theologians who took it upon themselves to refute the Deists. It seems that the theological climate was exceedingly bleak and religiously there was almost a vacuum.

Yet there was some compensation provided by the 'Religious Societies'. About 1676 a Dr. Horneck gathered together a group of young men in London who wished to apply themselves to good discourse and to edify themselves. Other groups grew out of the original one and a book, 'The Country Parson's Advice to his Parishioners', was published, which was highly prized by the members of the Holy Club under John Wesley's leadership. The meetings were to be made up of the reciting of liturgical prayers and the reading of books of practical divinity.[1] If time allowed a psalm might be sung and those who were so disposed might discourse with on another about their spiritual concerns. The Rule indicated that they should love one another, speak evil to no man,

---

[1]. From the life of Anthony Horneck in Hone's Lives of Eminent Christians I pp. 309, 310.

---

to pray if possible seven times a day, to keep close to the Church of England and to examine themselves everynight. Another kind of Society which was probably an offshoot from the Religious Societies was the formation of the Society for the Promotion of Christian Knowledge (1698). Its aim was to provide schools in London where the catechism could be taught to children not normally within the reach of the Church and to print good books for the poor.

Such was the Anglicanism, with its strengths and weaknesses in which John Wesley and the eighteenth century Methodists were nurtured. Yet it is plain that we cannot ascribe the development of Wesley's spiritual genius and the formation of his theology solely to the nurture and influence of his Church. He learned much from Thomas à Kempis and Jeremy Taylor's Holy Living and Holy Dying. But there were two strong eighteenth century influences playing upon him from outside the Church of England. In 1726 William Law published, 'A Treatise on Christian Perfection.' It is quite drastic in its demands for the renunciation by the Christian of all enjoyments and indulgences, such as the enjoyment of riches. The only purpose of riches is that we should use them to relieve the poor. In 1728 he published, 'A Serious Call to a devout and Holy Life' where Law makes it plain that he is not giving advice to cloistered saints but to ordinary people. All people are to live Christ-like lives. Zinzendorf (1700-60), a Moravian, organised religious societies in Saxony. Under Zinzendorf the communities sought to recapture the spirit and practice of the Agapé and hymn singing played a large part in their worship and life. They had a simple belief in immediate answers to prayer. It is easy to recognise some similarity between these Moravians and the early Methodists. One of the Moravian aims was the evangelisation of the heathen and it was in the pursuit of this aim that some of them met John Wesley and influenced his life.

It is against this background that it is now possible to consider Wesley's view of sin and his call to the people to search for perfect love.

CHAPTER TWO

WESLEY'S ANTHROPOLOGY

The nature of Man

Wesley finds that the natural man is dead to God and this is seen in the sermon on the, 'Circumcision of the heart' where he says, 'we are, of ourselves, all sin and vanity, that confusion of ignorance, and error reign over our understanding . . . . .'[1] Stress is laid on the corrupt state of natural man. In harmony with the Reformed outlook he insists on the total corruption of natural man basing this on the doctrine of original sin. A man's heart, he says, 'is altogether corrupt and abominable.'[2] He believes that all offspring of Adam are of their own nature inclined to evil and to be accounted righteous before God must be only for the merit of Christ by faith.

In The Minutes 1744 he explains how it is that Adam's sin can be imputed to the whole human race.

> 'In Adam all die, that is 1) our bodies then
> became mortal, 2) our souls died; that is were
> disunited from God. And hence 3) we are all
> born with a sinful, devilish nature. By reason
> whereof 4) we are children of wrath, liable to
> death eternal'.[3]

From this Wesley denies that natural man has free will or any power of his own to do good. These assumptions may be

---

1. The Circumcision of the Heart, 1733 Sermons I, p. 267.
2. Sermon of Salvation by Faith, 1738 Sermons I, p. 37f.
3. Minutes 1745 Works VIII, p. 285.

identified. The first is that natural man is totally corrupt, the second is that this corruption is the result of original sin and third that man can be justified only through God's grace in Christ. The Fall and the consequence are thus fundamental to Wesley's doctrine of justification. The righteousness of faith, Wesley says, pre-supposes that the man to whom it is given has been deprived of the image of God and been united by His wrath and that through sin, which has killed his soul, he now hastens to everlasting death. The Natural man is always represented as thoroughly corrupt. The innate corruption in his heart and innermost nature is described as an evil root from which spring both inward and outward sin.[1] Original and inbred sin, from which all other sin derives, is compared to a sour yeast which to some extent promotes all the movements of the soul and taints words, deeds and actions. This evil leads on to the thought of guilt. The punishment that man should receive is eternal damnation but when the mind turns to the relation to God the sins that fetter men are seen as debts.

In contrast to Pseudo-Dionysius who said that there was always part of the soul which was indestructible Wesley holds that by nature man is utterly depraved. The doctrine of original sin published in 1757 is an answer to John Taylor's book on original sin.[2] Before the Fall Wesley believed that man lived in a state of perfection and this is highlighted in this sermon on Justification of Faith.[3] The 'Imago Dei' was threefold. First there

---

1. The Way to the Kingdom, 1741, Sermon I p. 156f.
2. Works IX, p. 193.
3. Sermons, I p. 116.

was the natural image through which a man was immortal and had free will. He was also immune to pain. Second there was the political image which gave him the power of ruling over lowly creatures. Man's original perfection was most pronounced of all in his moral image, which meant that he was created in righteousness and holiness. Just as God is love so man is at first imbued with love. His whole being bore its imprint. Man had true knowledge of God and his work and lived on the intellectual plane proper to Him 'in the right state of his intellectual powers, and in his love, which is true holiness.'[1]

In the Fall the conditions of human life were reversed and primitive perfection was afforded by total corruption of man's nature. Through Adam men suffered spiritual, temporal and eternal death.[2] The 'Imago Dei' was not lost and man was now stamped with the image of the devil, with pride and self-will. Evil precedes bad nurture and Wesley cites the biblical dogma that Adam's sin is the cause of the fall of the race. In his connection between the Fall and corruption of man, (and here Wesley keeps close to St. Augustine in interpreting St. Paul's doctrine of original sin), Adam is regarded as the first ancestor and representative of mankind and his disobedience made all men sinners, for they were all 'in the loins of their first Parent, the common head and representative of them all.'[3]

---

[1]. The doctrine of original sin, Works IX p. 293.
[2]. The doctrine of original sin, Works IX p. 245.
[3]. Notes 1755, Romans 5 v 12, 14.

Original sin is sometimes described as an inclination to evil but Wesley uses stronger language, defining it as a total corruption of the value of human nature - a corruption manifested in atheism and idolatory, pride and self-will.

In his sermon on, 'Original sin' Wesley describes the doctrine of original sin as the fundamental difference between Christianity and paganism.

> 'But still as none of them were appraised of the fall of man, so none of them know of his total corruption. They knew not that all men were empty of all good, and fitted will all manner of evil. They were wholly ignorant of the entire deprivation of the whole human nature, of every man born into the world in every faculty of his soul, not so much by those particular vices which reign in particular persons as by the general flood of allusion and idolatry, of pride, self-will and love of the world.'[1]

For Wesley, then, original sin is not only the corruption inherent in man but it is also guilt. Since the Fall man is subject to guilt and punishment. This punishment is seen in suffering, which is the consequence of sin. It follows for Wesley that all are guilty for through their fellowship with Adam as the representative of the race, they share in his trespass. Before God, even children are not innocent but involved in the guilt of Adam's sin. Yet, Wesley maintains that although man is subject to guilt and punishment

---

[1]. Sermon on Original Sin 1760, Works VI p. 63.

because of his fellowship with Adam, he is nevertheless absolved
from original sin because of the atonement of Christ.[1]

It is important to grasp that Wesley never diverged from his
belief in the corruption of natural man for he believed that
original sin is the prime factor in human nature. We are all 'by
nature dead in sin and consequently children of wrath.'[2] The
doctrine of original sin is of fundamental importance in Wesley's
understanding of salvation. The Fall is regarded as the necessary
condition of the work of Christ and Wesley says it was the reason
of Christ's coming. The deprivation through Adam corresponds to
the restoration through Christ, although the work of the latter
surpasses that of the former. Just as Adam represents mankind in
his disobedience Christ is our representative in his work of
atonement. Because the whole of mankind is involved in guilt and
punishment man has no chance of saving himself by his own
efforts. Instead he is referred exclusively to God's grace in Christ
and in this way the doctrine of original sin safeguards the idea of
grace.

It is important to note Wesley's individualistic approach to
the doctrine of original sin as well as his collective one. This is of
course seen in the importance which he attaches to personal
experience. Therefore we find in his theology an interest in
psychological factors. Like the Moravians he puts the chief

---

1. Minutes 1744 Works VIII p. 277.
2. Short History of Methodism 1765 Works VIII p. 349.

emphasis on the awareness of sin rather than on sin as an objective fact. 'Feel that your carnal mind is enmity against God.'[1]

The process of salvation in the individual begins when he becomes conscious of his sinfulness with conviction of sin. Wesley says that no one can come to Christ as his Saviour until he knows and feels himself a lost sinner.

Original sin involves guilt but Wesley regards this guilt as imputed and not personal. Wesley found authority in the Bible for this distinction between personal sin and imputed guilt. Adam's sin is imputed to his children but they have no personal sin. All men are burdened with guilt but Adam's descendants cannot feel his sin to be theirs in quite the same way as Adam and Eve felt it. Alongside original guilt there is the idea of personal guilt, deriving from the actual sin of the individual. The descendants of Adam cannot choose for themselves, their guilt is only hereditary guilt. It is a guilt which is imputed to them but it is not personal. No one, says Wesley, is finally damned unless he chooses to be so. Wesley maintains that through Adam all mankind is implicated in sin and guilt and he emphasises the complete inability of man to attain salvation by himself. It can only come to him through faith. He also maintains that sin has been transmitted from Adam to his children.

If Wesley believes that man's nature is totally corrupt - can man have any real choice? He says that original sin does not

---

[1]. Works XI p. 180.

necessarily lead to actual sin and if man takes advantage of God's grace he can conquer the inclination to evil. Wesley finds that the opportunity for choice is based upon the foundation of grace.

Inward sins and outward sins

In the sermon on the 'Doctrine of Original Sin'[1] the specific sins which proceed from original sin are compared to evil sprouts proceeding from the same evil root. Sin is regarded as an organic relation between the root, the branches and the leaves. The inward sins are those of pride, wrath and foolish desire which are to be identified with seeking happiness in the creation instead of in God. These sins grow like a root of bitterness and darken the soul of the man who was previously in a state of grace by which God wishes to preserve him. After inward sin, faith and love disappear. The man commits outward sin. In the sermon on 'The great privilege of those that are born of God' Wesley sets out the progress from grace to sin in eight stages.

> '1. The divine seed of loving, conquering faith, remains in him that is born of God. He keepeth himself by the grace of God and cannot commit sin.
>
> 2. A temptation arises whether from the world, the flesh or the devil, it matters not.
>
> 3. The Spirit of God gives him warning that sin is near and bids him more abundantly watch with prayer.

---

1. 1757 Works IX p. 433.

4. He gives way, in some degree, to the
   temptation which now begins to grow
   pleasing to him.

5. The Holy Spirit is grieved, his faith is
   weakened and his love of God grows cold.

6. The spirit reproves him more sharply and
   saith, 'This is the way, walk thou in it.'

7. He turns away from the painful voice of
   God and listens to the pleasing voice of
   the tempter.

8. Evil desire begins and spreads in his soul,
   till faith and love vanish away: He is then
   capable of committing outward sin, the
   power of the Lord being departed from
   him.'[1]

In describing these stages in the process of sin by which
man falls from grace, Wesley attributes the responsibility to the
individual. The specific sins derive from the sinfulness in man's
nature and this corruption is regarded as the seed of all other sins.
As is seen in the 'Doctrine of Original Sin'[2] it is the cause of all
specific sins both in our hearts and lives.

The meaning of sin

Wesley, as is to be seen from his Sermon on the Mount[3], is
fond of describing sin as an injury, as corruption, as disease. He
pictures original sin as leprosy infecting mankind and the sins
proceeding from it as wounds and diseases. As sin is therefore
looked upon as an illness, salvation is called a healing - man is

---

1. Sermon on the Great Privilege of those that are born of God 1748 Works V p. 231.
2. Doctrine of Original Sin 1757 Works IX p. 462.
3. Sermon on the Mount I 1748 Works V p. 253.

cured of his inherent sinfulness as of disease. With sin seen in
this way, as the background of salvation and the motivation of its
indispensability, it is natural that the idea of sanctification should
come to the fore.

> 'And who might not say upon this supposition,
> 'I cannot see that we have much need of
> Christianity?' Nay not any at all, for they that
> are alive have no need of a Physician and the
> Christian Revelation speaks of nothing else
> but the great Physician of the souls nor can
> Christian Philosophy, whatever be thought of
> the Pagan, be more properly defined than in
> Plato's works: 'It is the only true method of
> healing a distempered soul.' But what need of
> this if we are in perfect health? If we are not
> diseased we do not want to cure. If we are
> not sick why should we seek for medicine to
> heal our sickness? What room is there to talk
> of our being renewed in 'knowledge' or
> 'holiness' after the image wherein we are
> created, if we never have lost that image? If
> we are as knowing and holy now, nay, far
> more so than Adam was immediately after his
> creation? If we take away this foundation
> that man is by nature foolish and sinful, fallen
> short of the glorious image of God, the
> Christian system falls at once, nor will it
> deserve so honourable an appellation as that
> of a 'cunningly devised fable.'[1]

Therefore no man can come to Christ the Physician before he is
conscious of his disease. This knowledge in man of the depravity
of his nature is the extreme subjective condition of his
sanctification. It is regarded as the first step in the process of
salvation in which the goal is sanctification. Wesley speaks of the
great Physician of the Souls applying medicines to heal the

---

[1]. The Doctrine of Original Sin 1757 Work IX p. 194.

sickness; for Christ loved us and gave himself for us. Through repentance and lowliness of heart the deadly disease of pride is healed, that of self-will be resignation, a meek and thankful submission to the will of God, and for the love of the world in all its branches, the love of God is to renew man's heart in the image of God, to make good the total loss of righteousness and holiness. Man must learn the nature of his disease and how it can be cured. Inherent sin can be regarded as an illness which must be cured. It is important to recognise that for Wesley healing lies not only in liberation from sin but also from objective guilt. In the Sermon on the Fall of Man we read:

> 'Here is the remedy provided for all our guilt.
> He bore all our sins in his body on the tree.'[1]

The medical analogy to which Wesley seem to attach great importance can be applied not only to inherent sin but also to guilt. That it could is evidence of the great influence exercised by the idea of sanctification on his doctrine of salvation as a whole.

Grace

In the doctrine of Original Sin it can be seen that man's natural and political image have not been entirely lost.

> 'The image of God in which Adam was created,
> consisted eminently in righteousness and true
> holiness. But that part of the image of God
> which remained after the fall and remains in
> all men to this day is the natural image of
> God, namely the spiritual nature and
> immortality of the soul, not excluding the

---

1. Sermon on the Fall of Man 1788 Works VI, p. 223.

political image of God, or a degree of dominion
over the creatures still remaining.'[1]

Man has fallen but still retains

'an immaterial principle, a spiritual nature
endured with understanding and affections
and a degree of liberty of a self-moving, yes,
and self-governing power.'[2]

Although Wesley maintains that man is totally corrupt he also
maintains that God gives to all men his prevenient grace. Natural
man is devoid of free will yet all men have been endowed by
supernatural intervention with a measure of free will and some
power of discernment. The liberty given to man is a liberty
founded on grace. Grace is not irresistible for man can either co-
operate with it or oppose it. It is only through the grace of God
that man becomes capable of turning to Christ and believing in
Him. In the Doctrine of Original Sin we see that it is prevenient
grace which in varying degrees is given to everyone and makes it
possible for man, despite his natural condition, to seek God.[3]
Prevenient grace confers some discernment on everyone although
natural man as such lacks all knowledge of God. This discernment
comes to man through what is termed 'natural conscience'.
Wesley here agrees with St. Paul in Romans that even the
heathens are not without knowledge of God and his law.[4] This
discernment is not something which emanates from natural man's
own resources but derives from prevenient grace. The light given
to men by prevenient grace is associated with conscience and its

1. Doctrine of Original Sin, Works IX p. 381.
2. Sermon on the Heavenly Treasure in Earthen Vessels 1798 Works VII
   p.345.
3. Doctrine of Original Sin, Works IX p. 265.
4. Roman I v 19.

workings.   For Wesley conscience is an expression of prevenient grace.

> 'For allowing that all the souls of man are
> dead in sin by nature, this excuses none,
> seeing there is no man that is in a state of
> mere nature: There is no man, unless he has
> quenched the Spirit that is wholly void of the
> grace of God. No man living is entirely
> destitute of what is vulgarly called natural
> conscience. But this is not natural, it is more
> properly termed, preventing grace.   Every
> man has a greater or less measure of this,
> which waiteth not for the call of man.'[1]

In the Sermon Working out our own salvation Wesley says,

> 'Salvation begins with what is usually termed
> preventing grace, including the first wish to
> please God, the first down of light concerning
> his will and the first slight transient
> conviction of having sinned against him.   "All
> these imply some tendency toward life, some
> degree of salvation, the beginning of a
> deliverance from a blind, unfeeling heart,
> quite insensible of God and the things of God.'[2]

Thus it is with prevenient grace that salvation in the widest sense begins.

When we combine Wesley's doctrine of original sin with his view of prevenient grace we see that man becomes entirely dependant upon God for salvation and there is no possibility of such a thing as human merit. Equally clear is that this individualistic approach and the idea of prevenient grace on which this view is based implies a very strong emphasis on man's personal responsibility.

---

1. Sermon on Conscience 1988 Works VII p. 187f.
2. Sermon 'On Working out our own Salvation' 1788, Works VI, p. 509.

CHAPTER THREE

ATONEMENT, JUSTIFICATION AND SANCTIFICATION

Atonement

In the letter of 7th February 1778 Wesley speaks of the centrality of the atonement in Christianity:

> 'Indeed nothing in the Christian system is of greater consequence than the doctrine of Atonement. It is properly the distinguishing point between Deism and Christianity. Here then we divide - give up the Atonement, and the Deists are agreed with us.'[1]

Therefore it is important to begin with Wesley's view of the atonement as both justification and sanctification are based upon it. For Wesley Christ's work of atonement became the sole basis of justification and regeneration. Justifying faith became a faith in Christ's work of atonement and His merits. Thus Christ's work of atonement came to be regarded as the sole ground of human justification. Justification cannot be based on any righteousness in man himself - neither righteousness of outward acts nor righteousness of inward temper. Thus sanctification becomes not a cause but an effort of justification. Faith alone is regarded as the necessary condition for justification.

In his view of Atonement Wesley subscribes to the thirty-nine articles and the homilies of the Anglican Church. Three articles of the thirty-nine deal with Christ's work of atonement. In connection with the Incarnation it is maintained that Christ,

---

[1]. Letters VI p. 297f.

who was a true God and a true man, truly suffered, was crucified, dead and buried to reconcile his Father to us and to be a sacrifice not only for original guilt but also for all actual sins of men. The sacrifice of Christ once made is that perfect redemption, propitiation and satisfaction for all the sins of the whole world, both original and actual, and there is no other satisfaction of sin but that alone. In the article on justification, Christ's merits are said to be the only basis of human justification. Wesley agreed with the Articles in connection with the doctrine of the work of Christ as satisfaction and in the related idea of the merits of Christ. It was through the sin of Adam, who was not only the father but the representative of mankind, that all became subject to sin and punishment; similarly Christ, as the second Adam and representative of the human race, bore the sin of all. He suffered on behalf of all and his sacrifice was a full, perfect and sufficient satisfaction for the sins of the whole world. Man has no means of making satisfaction to the justice of God for his sins. The only hope is the vicarious suffering of Christ.

It was also important to Wesley that Christ's death should have an objective import with relation to God. Christ's work of atonement is also seen as the payment of ransom. Man cannot pay the debt he owes to God. Christ was a ransom for us all and a sacrifice to God. His work acquired satisfactional and meritorious significance for all men. In "The Sermon on God's Love to Fallen Man"[1] it is seen that Grace has its place in Wesley's idea of atonement too. Salvation on the grounds of man's own merits; and

---

[1]. Sermon on God's Love to Fallen Man 1788 Works VI, p. 239.

as the former is the true way the stress is laid on grace. Again Wesley sees the concept of Christ's work of atonement as an act of deliverance and conquest. The atonement is a step in which God no longer puts forth His wrath but instead appears as a loving Father.

Yet it is important to stress that the characteristic expression of the idea of atonement lies for Wesley in satisfaction. He links the atonement with Christ's office as High Priest which as well as His vicarious work of atonement, also comprises His intercession with the Father on man's behalf. The victorious and liberating aspect of Christ's work finds the expression primarily in his office as king.

Justification

Wesley's understanding of the Atonement is the foundation of justification and sanctification. Man is justified by faith because of Christ's atonement. His sins are forgiven and he is accepted by God. Justification is linked with Christ's work as High Priest. In Wesley's sermon "Justification by Faith"[1] there is given an insight into the meaning of justification. The plain scriptural notion of justification is pardon, the forgiveness of sins. It is that act of God the Father whereby, for the sake of the propitiation made by the blood of His Son, He shows forth his righteousness by the remission of the sins that are past. To him that is justified or forgiven God will not impute sin to his condemnation. He will not

---

[1]. Justification by Faith, Sermons I, p. 119ff.

condemn him on that account. His sins, all his past sins in thought, word and deed are covered, are blotted out, shall not be remembered or mentioned against him any more than if they had not been. God will not inflict on that sinner what he deserves to suffer because the Son of His love has suffered for him. From the time we are accepted He loves, blesses and watches over us for good even as if we had never sinned.

Wesley then continues to ask, 'who are they that are justified?' The answer, following St. Paul, is clear - it is the ungodly. It is only sinners that have any occasion for pardon, it is sin alone which admits of being forgiven. It is our unrighteousness to which the pardoning God is merciful and it is our iniquity which he remembers no more. It is not a saint but a sinner that is forgiven, and under the notion of a sinner. God justifies not the godly but the ungodly, not those that are already holy but the unholy. Christ as the Good Shepherd pardons those who need his pardoning mercy. He saves from the guilt of sin sinners of every kind, of every degree, men who until then were ungodly, in whom the love of the Father was not and consequently in whom dwelt no good thing. Those who are sick, the burden of whose sins is intolerable, are they that need a Physician; those who are guilty, who groan under the wrath of God, are they that need a pardon. Those who are condemned already, not only by God but also by their own conscience, as by a thousand witnesses, cry aloud for him that justifies the ungodly through the redemption that is in Jesus. Wesley has a sharp answer to those who say that before a man is justified he may feed the hungry or clothe the naked and do other good works. He says that these are

in a sense 'good works' before he is justified but it does not
strictly follow that they are good in themselves or good in the
sight of God. All truly good works, says Wesley, follow after
justification and they are good and acceptable to God in Christ
because they spring out of a true and living faith. By a purity of
reason, says Wesley, all works done before justification are not
good in the Christian sense forasmuch as they do not spring of
faith in Christ.

Wesley's argument is as follows.

No works are good which are not done as God has willed and
commanded them to be done. But no works done before
justification are done as God has willed and commanded them to
be done. Therefore, no works done before justification are good.
Wesley says that none of our works can be done in love while the
love of God as our Father is not in us; and this love cannot be in us
until we receive the spirit of adoption. Man, says Wesley, is
justified by faith. Faith in general is a divine supernatural
evidence or conviction of things not seen, not discoverable by our
bodily senses as being either past, future of spiritual. Justifying
faith implies not only a divine evidence or conviction that God was
in Christ reconciling the world to himself but a sure trust and
confidence that Christ died for my sins, that he loved me and gave
himself for me.

Wesley describes the nature of this faith as a sure trust and
confidence that God has and will forgive our sins and that he has
accepted us again into his favour for the merits of Christ's death
and passion. By affirming that this faith is the term of or

condition of justification Wesley says there is no justification without it. So long as we are without this faith we are strangers and aliens.

Faith is therefore the necessary condition - the only necessary condition - of justification. As on the one hand a man should have everything else without faith yet he cannot be justified, so on the other hand, though he is supposed to want everything else, yet if he has faith he cannot but justified. When a sinner, helpless and hopeless, casts himself wholly on the mercy of God in Christ no one can doubt that he is forgiven. Faith is in this sense the sure condition of justification. A person who comes to God by faith must fix his eye on his own wickedness, on his guilt and helplessness, without having the least regard to any supposed good in himself, to any virtue or righteousness. He must come, says Wesley, as a mere sinner, inwardly and outwardly, self-destroyed and self-condemned, bringing nothing to God but ungodliness pleading nothing of his own but sin and misery.

Wesley considered that in his doctrine of justification he was in full harmony with the attitude of the Reformation. In his University Sermon on "Salvation by Faith"[1] he emphasises his agreement with Luther. His view of justification is bound up with his view of man and doctrine of justification by faith without the works of the law was clearly a natural consequence. As it is seen from his sermon and typical of this justifying faith, is a personal

---

[1]. Salvation by Faith, Sermons I, p. 51.

trust in the efficacy of Christ's work for mankind. This trust is above all a trust in the atonement of Christ.

The opposition between the way of the law and the way of faith is particularly strongly stressed in the time after the evangelical revolution in his doctrine of justification. Wesley uses the idea which is typical of Calvinist Theology - that of the two covenants, the covenant of works and the covenant of grace which he writes about in his sermon on the "Righteousness of Faith"[1]. In this sermon he maintains that the conditions under which God gave man the covenant of works are quite different from those pertaining to the covenant of grace. The covenant of work was given in Paradise and required man's perfect and unfailing obedience and it was necessary for man to remain in that state of perfection in which he was created. The covenant of grace was established through Christ with fallen man. The covenant of works was not established by man but by Adam in paradise. The covenant of grace was established by God through Christ immediately afterwards. This was partly manifested after Adam's fall, in the promise in Genesis III v 15 and it was revealed rather more clearly to Abraham (Genesis XXII v 16, 18) and still more clearly to David and the prophets. With Christ the gospel was fully revealed. The aim of fallen man is to regain the grace and life of God. In the sermon "The Marks of the New Birth"[2], justifying faith is seen as a result of man's total inability to attain justification by his own works. Man must abandon all reliance on his own works and put his trust solely in the atonement of Christ.

---

1. Righteousness of Faith, 1746, Sermons I, p. 132ff.
2. The Marks of the New Birth, 1748, Sermons I, p. 284f.

In "Satan's Devices"[1] a man may not plead any sanctity or works of his own as grounds for acceptance, nor need anything of the kind precede this.

In the "Principles of a Methodist"[2] Wesley lays emphasis on repentance before justification and its fruits. At the Conference in 1744 he declared that, although faith is said to be the condition of justification, there must be repentance before justification, which implies the conviction of sin and the corresponding works. In the Minutes of 1745 he says that the fruits of this repentance ought also to precede faith.[3]

This subject is also explored in "A further appeal to Men of Reason and Religion"[4], where Wesley urges the importance of repentance for justification. Faith alone justifies and repentance and its fruits are not necessary in the same degree. The fruits of repentance are only conditionally necessary, i.e. if there is time and opportunity. The emphasis upon the fruits of repentance sprang out of Wesley's struggle with Quietism. The Quietists, strong in France and Spain in the 16th and 17th centuries, laid great stress on the passive nature of man. Vocal and mental prayer were to be discouraged and pure love was to exclude all self-interest. Wesley strongly disagreed with this and the antinomianism which sprang from it.

---

[1]. Satan's Devices, 1750, Sermons II, p. 194.
[2]. Principles of a Methodist, 1742, Works VIII, p. 361.
[3]. Minutes, 1745, Works VIII, p. 281f.
[4]. 1745, Works VIII, p. 56f.

Justification to Sanctification

Wesley distinguishes between justification and sanctification although the two are closely associated. Sanctification begins in man with the new birth and implies a real inherent fruit of justification but also a distinct gift of God and of a different nature. In the sermon on "Justification by Faith"[1] justification is defined as 'what God does for us by his Spirit'. Justification involves a relative change and sanctification a real change. In Justification there is an objective change where there is a transformation in the relation between man and God with the result that man is now possessed of God's favour. There is deliverance from the guilt of sin. Sanctification is a subjective change, a real renewal in man himself and there is liberation from the power and root of sin. Justification restores us to God's favour and takes away our guilt and sanctification restores us to the image of God and is concerned with taking away the power of sin. Although they take place at the same time they are regarded as distinct and in this Wesley diverges from Luther to whom justification also included inward renewal. For Wesley, the Christian life becomes two focal points: justification or the forgiveness of sins and the ethical regeneration of sanctification.

In the sermon on "Salvation by Faith"[2] Wesley maintains the importance of the New Birth and stresses that Salvation which comes by faith is a salvation from both the power and guilt of sin. In the New Birth, a new life is accorded to those who believe in

---

1. Justification by Faith, 1746, Sermons I, p. 119.
2. Salvation by Faith, 1738, Sermons I, p. 41f.

Christ and this life will grow and develop towards perfection. Saving faith naturally produces good works.

The importance of sanctification in Wesley's view of salvation is seen in the sermon "The Law established through Faith"[1] where faith becomes the means of which love is the end. Faith is only the handmaid of love. Only love is the end of all the commandments of God. In the Sermon 'The Lord our righteousness' the real purpose of the imputation of the righteousness of Christ is thus declared to be the sanctification of man[2]. The idea of sanctification is of paramount importance in Wesley's description of a Christian where he says that sanctity is regarded as an ethical transformation of the heart and life of man. Its essence is love and being a Christian means having faith which is active in love. A person who believes in Christ walks in the Holy Spirit and in him are revealed the fruits of the spirit. He sees Christianity from the point of view of new birth and sanctification.

In the "Ernest Appeal" he says that religion is love - 'the love of God and of all mankind, the loving God with all our heart, and soul and strength, as having first loved us, as the fountain of all the good we have received, and of all we ever hope to enjoy; and the loving every soul which God hath made, every man on earth as our own soul'[3]. Religion is regarded as God's method of healing a soul and the renewal of man in the image of God becomes the end of religion.

---

[1]. The Law Established Through Faith, 1750, Sermons II, p. 77f.

[2]. The Lord our Righteousness 1765, Sermons II, p. 439.

[3]. An Ernest Appeal, 1743, Works VIII, p. 3.

CHAPTER 4

THE STAGES IN THE SPIRITUAL PROGRESS

The two basic features of Wesley and Methodism - revivalism and conversion - have been exaggerated at the expense of all else. Yet when Wesley's doctrine of salvation is analysed it becomes evident that Wesley saw salvation as a gradual development. Salvation is seen as a process by which man passes through a series of successive stages and each stage represents a different and higher level. Wesley uses the word salvation in two different ways. In the "Minutes 1746" it is used to signify Christian Salvation proper - both present and final salvation - salvation at its inception, continuation and conclusion[1]. Secondly it is used in a wider sense which comprises justification and sanctification and the emphasis in "A Farther Appeal" is on Sanctification[2].

> 'By Salvation I mean, not barely, according
> to the vulgar notion, deliverance from hell,
> or going to heaven, but a present
> deliverance from sin, a restoration of the
> soul to its primitive health, its original
> purity, a recovery of the divine nature, the
> renewal of our souls after the image of God,
> in righteousness and true holiness, in
> justice, mercy, and truth. This implies all
> holy and heavenly tempers, and, by
> consequence all holiness of conversion.'

---

1. Minutes, 1746, Works VIII, p. 290.
2. A Farther Appeal, 1745, Works VIII, p. 47.

This salvation begins with the efforts of prevenient grace and includes the whole of the later process of salvation which ends in glorification.

Like St. John of the Cross, Wesley places the beginning of the Christian Life in man at baptism. In baptism the child is freed from its guilt and re-born before it can enter into fellowship with God. Baptism is said to be the ordinary instrument of our justification and by it we enter into convenant with God and are admitted into the Church. Yet the grace accorded to man in baptism can be learnt and so Wesley preaches that man must be born again. The emphasis is on the New Birth instead of on baptism. Baptism is a human act and the New Birth is a change wrought by God in the soul. Not all the baptised experience the New Birth.

The order of salvation according to Wesley is described in his sermon "The Spirit of Bondage and Adoption" 1746. Man is described in three states:

First: The state of a 'natural man'

The characteristics of the 'natural man' are identified as follows: He is in a state of stress, his spiritual senses are not awake and they desire neither spiritual good or evil. The eyes of his understanding are closed and he is utterly ignorant of God. He is a stranger to the law of God. Because he is asleep he is in some sense of rest. Because he is blind he is also secure. He does not see that he stands on the edge of the pit and he does not fear. He is secure because he is utterly ignorant of himself. This ignorance is seen in the men of learning. He reads and argues and proves that every man may do as he will. From the ignorance of himself and God there may sometimes arise a kind of joy in congratulating himself upon his own wisdom and goodness. Because of this he feels he is walking in great liberty. yet all this time he is the servant of sin. He commits sin yet he is not tested.

Second: The State of one who is 'under the law'

God touches the heart of the man that sleeps in darkness and by degrees the eyes of his understanding are opened. The inward spiritual meaning of law of God now begins to glare upon him. He feels that the wages of sin are death and the pleasing dream ends and joy vanishes. He feels the origin of a worried spirit and truly desires to break loose from sin begins to struggle with it. The more he strains, wishes and labours to be free, the more he feels his chains. The whole struggle, Wesley says, is described in Romans Chapter 7. In his treatment of the law, Wesley could not agree with the dualistic view of Luther. In "The Spirit of Bondage and of Adoption"[1] the law is always regarded as holy and good. Thus he expressly repudiates Luther's belief that it can be ranged with sin, death and the devil. In the "Journal" Wesley writes:

> 'Again how blasphemously does he
> (Luther) speak of good works and of the
> law of God - constantly coupling the law
> with sin, death, hell or the devil and
> teaching that Christ delivers us from them
> alike. Whereas it can no more be proved by

---

[1]. Spirit of Bondage and Adoption, 1746, Sermons I, p. 189f.

Scripture that Christ delivers us from the
law of God than that He delivers us from
holiness or from heaven."[1]

Third: The one who is 'under grace'

This state is of one who has found grace or favour in the sight of
God and his eyes are opened in quite a different manner than
before to see a loving gracious God. Healing light breaks out upon
his soul and he sees the light of the glorious love of God in the face
of Jesus Christ. Here ends both the guilt and power of sin, remorse
and sorrow of heart. Where the Spirit is, there is liberty from sin
and man fights and conquers.

These three states - the natural, legal and evangelical - are
often mingled together and in some measure meet in one and the
same person. The legal is often mingled with the natural state and
the evangelical with the legal. Wesley takes his stand against the
Moravians declaring that there are degrees of faith:

> 'There are degrees in faith, and that a man
> may have some degree of it before all
> things become new - before he has the full
> answer of faith, the abiding witness of the
> Spirit or the clear perception that Christ
> dwelleth in him.'[2]

In the above description the difference between the new birth and
entire sanctification does not find expression, the regenerate man
being sometimes presented as completely sanctified. Later,

---

[1]. Journal, 15th July, 1741.
[2]. Journal, 31st December, 1739, J. II, p. 329.

however, the distinction between new birth and entire sanctification, which was indeed never entirely absent even during the earliest evangelical period,[1] is clearly stated. The Sanctification is described as an organic development - the believer growing from a child to a young man.

It is difficult to set out an order of salvation in detail according to Wesley. In the "Explanatory Notes upon the New Testament 1755", the order is presented in the following way: 1) Bondage to sin; 2) The knowledge of sin by the law - inward death; 3) The revelation of the righteousness of God in Christ through the gospel; 4) The centre of all, faith, embracing that righteousness; 5) Justification whereby God forgives all past sin and freely accepts the sinner; 6) The gift of the Holy Spirt: a sense of God's love: new inward life; 7) The free service of righteousness.

A detailed account of the way of salvation is to be found in Wesley's sermon called "The Scripture Way of Salvation"[2] with the text 'Ye are saved through faith' Ephesians 2 v 8. Wesley defines salvation as the entire work of God, from the dawning of grace in the soul until it is consumated in glory. Wesley describes justification as pardon - the forgiveness of sins. At the same time as a man is justified sanctification begins. In that instant we are born of the Spirit. There is a real as well as a relative change. Relative change involves liberation from the guilt of sin and real change is the liberation from the inherent power of sin. In this state sin is only suspended and not destroyed. They feel the flesh

1. Sermons, 'Almost Christian'.
2. VI, 1765, Sermons II, p. 445.

lusting against the spirit - nature opposing the grace of God. From the time of being born again the gradual work of sanctification takes place. Wesley goes on to define faith as divine evidence and conviction. Faith is the condition of justification and without faith no man is justified. There is a repentance consequent upon as well as a repentance previous to justification. Repentance and the practice of all good works - works of piety, as well as works of mercy - are in some sense necessary to sanctification. The repentance consequent upon justification implies no guilt, no sense of condemnation, no consciousness of the wrath of God. It is properly a conviction of the sin which still remains in our heart. Wesley then speaks of the gradual proceeding work of sanctification until the soul is pure from every spot of sin - it is clean from all unrighteousness.

With this background it is now possible to suggest the stages in the process of salvation according to Wesley. In the widest sense sanctification can be said to begin with the operation in man of prevenient grace. In the sermon on the "Scripture Way of Salvation", grace 'comprises all the drawings of the Father - the desires after God which , if we yield to them increase more and more.'[1] The workings of grace imply some degree of salvation of man moving from a deliverance from sin towards God. The first real step on the way to salvation according to Wesley is grace, which is the repentance before justification. This, which has been seen, involves conviction of sin. In the "Sermon on the Mount" it is also described as 'incipient poverty of the Spirit'[2]. In this, there is

---

1. Scripture Way of Salvation, 1765, Sermons II, p. 445.
2. Sermon on the Mount 1, 1748, Sermons I, p. 232.

gradual development in man as he can deepen his sense of repentance. The test of whether repentance is meaningful is to be seen in the fruits. Repentance should lead to real desires and sincere resolutions of amendment. Also a man forgives his brother and ceases to do what is evil and seeks to do good. There then follows justification and New Birth which are bestowed upon a person in a single instant. In Chapter three justification was identified as a relative change and the New Birth as a real change. Although the forgiveness of sins takes place at the same time with the New Birth nevertheless they are to be distinguished. At New Birth a man is freed from the power of sin while God's love flows into his heart. At this time also a man may feel assurance where he becomes aware of God's love for him and that he is now reconciled.

The stages in Wesley's view of sanctification are to be seen as he identifies that another repentance and faith are necessary for growth after justification and New Birth. In the sermon on "Sin in Believers" the will of man is not yet subordinated to the will of God[1]. During this stage man is aware of his sin and of his inability to do good on the basis of his own resources. At this stage awareness of sin is accompanied by consciousness of acceptance by God. In the sermon on the "Scripture Way of Salvation" it is seen that this repentance is seen in its fruits.

> 'First all works of piety, such as public
> prayer, family prayer, and praying in the
> closet, receiving the supper of the Lord,
> searching the scriptures by hearing,

---

[1]. On Sin in Believers, 1763, Sermons II, p. 372f.

> reading, meditating, and using such a
> measure of fostering or abstinence as our
> bodily health allows.
>
> 'Secondly, all works of mercy, whether they
> relate to the bodies or souls of men, such as
> feeding the hungry, clothing the naked,
> entertaining the stranger, visiting those
> that are in prison, or sick or variously
> afflicted. These are the fruits meet for
> repentance which are necessary for
> sanctification. This is the way wherein God
> hath appointed his children to wait for
> complete salvation.'[1]

Without a knowledge of one's sin, repentance or good works man cannot be fully sanctified. Obedience is necessary to the development of the Christian life. This obedience in good works is seen as a kind of active waiting. Yet it is faith rather than good works which is of absolute necessity to growth in the spiritual life.

Eventually one is led to a higher stage in the new life, that of complete sanctification or Christian perfection. When a man has been freed by the New Birth from the power of sin, he is freed from the root of sin as well by complete sanctification and all sin is washed away. Yet there still remains some imperfection and this is the negative side of Christian perfection. In a positive sense it is perfect love. Even within Christian perfection there is further development. There is no perfection 'which does not admit of a continual increase'[2]. The gradual development still continues and it is conceived as growth in love.

---

[1]. Scripture Way of Salvation, 1765, Sermons II, p. 445.

[2]. Sermon on Christian Perfection, 1750, Sermons II, p. 156.

'Forgetting the things that are behind the
reaching forward into those that are before,
press on to the mark, for the prize of your
high calling of God in Christ Jesus.'[1]

The final stage in man's spiritual progress reaches its climax
in entire sanctification. This is final justification or final salvation
and glorification beyond the grave. Therefore it is to be seen that
Wesley's process of salvation takes the form of an ascent by steps.
At the risk of over-simplification we may set it out thus:
Repentance or conviction, justification including the New Birth,
sanctification in the sense of Christian perfection and glorification.
This ascent is based upon his belief that there are degrees of good
and evil - of enmity to God, self-denial, peace, joy and love.
Inward and outward holiness of merit can be expressed in
degrees. In 'Farther Thoughts on Christian Perfection' Wesley
imagines a development towards ever greater perfection even
after death. Question 29 asks 'Can those who are perfect grow in
grace?' and the answer is 'undoubtedly they can, and that not only
while they are in the body but to all eternity.'[2]

It would be wrong to compare Wesley's degrees with the
Spiritual exercises of Ignatius and yet this comparison does gain
force from Wesley's application of the 'Ascent' to the organisation
of the Methodist Societies so that it becomes something of a rule.
The societies were divided into classes of about twelve persons
and each class had a leader. From 'Thoughts upon Methodism'[3] it
is to be seen that members belonged to one or other of these

1. Sermon on Faith, 1788, Works VII, p. 282.
2. Works XL, p. 426.
3. Thoughts upon Methodism, Works XIII, p. 226.

groups according to their spiritual state and experience. Three
such groups may be identified. Firstly, for those who had a mild
interest in the faith and who wanted to meet socially. The leaders
received the weekly contribution - which became known as class
money - and fulfilled a pastoral role. If any walked disorderly
they were quickly discovered and either amended or were
dismissed. Those receiving the exercises of Ignatius were divided
into three groups. The first group may correspond with Wesley's.
These people according to Ignatius were those desiring only to be
instructed in the ordinary duties of a Christian life and to set their
consciences at rest by a good confession. Many would be illiterate
and lacking in depth of character or natural capacity from whom
not much fruit can be expected[1]. In Wesley's 'Thoughts upon
Methodism' we read:

> 'For those who knew in whom they had believed
> there was another help provided. Five or six,
> either married or single men, met together at
> such an hour as was convenient, according to the
> direction of St. James, 'Confess your faults one to
> another, and pray one for another, and ye shall
> be healed'. And five or six of the married or
> single women met together for the same purpose.
> Innumerate blessings have attended this
> institution, especially in those who were going on
> to perfection.'[2]

Annotation XIX of the Exercises of Ignatius speaks of a second
group of people which can correspond with Wesley's group
described above. These people were both educated and had the

[1]. W.H. Longridge. The Spiritual exercises of St. Loyola Annotation 18, p. 17.
[2]. Thoughts upon Methodism, Works XIII, p. 226.

capacity for growth in the Christian Life but were hindered by external duties and business[1].

Wesley speaks of a third grouping, 'When any seemed to have attained this (i.e. perfection) they were allowed to meet with a select number who appeared so far as man could judge, to be partakers of the same 'great salvation'.[2]

Annotation XX of Ignatius's exercises speaks of a third class comprising those who have both education and capacity to learn and who are free from external hindrances.[3] Thus we see similarity in the classification of groups. It is more difficult to draw similarities between the content which was to be discussed. Ignatius had a well defined plan and one set of exercises led to another in a sequence which may be compared with programmed learning today. Yet upon examination it is possible to identify a similarity between the particular and general examination of conscience which was basic for all three groups of people according to Ignatius and the 'Rules of the Band of Wesley Societies'. The particular examination according to St. Ignatius was the examination of the soul which was to be made daily. The person ought to resolve to guard himself carefully against the particular sin or defect which he desires to correct and amend. He is to ask for grace to remember how often he has fallen into that particular sin or defect and to amend it in the future.[4]

1. W.H. Longridge, The Spiritual exercises of St. Loyola. Annotation x19 p.20.
2. Thoughts upon Methodism. Works XIII. p.227.
3. W.H. Longridge, The Spiritual exercises of St. Loyola. Annotation XX, p.20.
4. W.H. Longridge, The Spiritual exercises of St. Loyola. p.44.

In Wesley's 'Rules of the Band Societies'[1] there are set out a number of questions which are to be asked which are similar to the particular examination of Ignatius.

'Have you the forgiveness of your sins?
Have you peace with God?
Has no sin, inward or outward, dominion over you?
Do you desire to be told of your faults?
What known sins have you committed since our last meeting?
What temptations have you met with?
How were you delivered?'[2]

Therefore some resemblance may be seen between rules for the Methodist Societies and the Annotations 18-20 of Ignatius's exercises.

Thus it is to be seen that sanctification lies between justification and final salvation. It includes the whole process of recovery, the object of which is to restore man to the image of God. This is the proper use of the word sanctification and it is obviously a gradual development. The gradual process is interrupted by the direct intervention of God which in a single instant raises man to a higher plane. It is this continuation of the gradual and the instantaneous that characterises Wesley's view of salvation so that it is important to guard against any reading of his work that would make his view of salvation one or other of these possibilities.

---

[1]. Rules of the Band Societies, Works XIII, p. 272.
[2]. Rules of the Band Societies, Works XIII, pp. 272-3.

CHAPTER FIVE

CHRISTIAN PERFECTION

The idea of Christian Perfection was central to Wesley's belief and an important stage in spiritual progress. It is mentioned in sermons, letters, journals and in the hymns that were published by the Wesley brothers. In a letter, he writes, 'This doctrine is the grand depositum which God has lodged with the people called Methodists; and for the sake of propagating this chiefly He appeared to have raised us up.'[1] The whole idea of Christian perfection must be seen against the background of the preceding chapters - Wesley's doctrine of man, the importance of sin, justification and sanctification.

a) Wesley's view on perfection

Wesley's views on perfection are expounded in (i) the sermon on Christian Perfection and (ii) 'a plain account of Christian perfection.'

(i) The sermon on Christian Perfection (1740) is based upon the text in Philippines 3 v 12, 'Not that I have already obtained this or am already perfect'. Wesley says that the word 'perfect' is what many people cannot bear. The very sound of it is an abomination to them. Yet he claims that it is not possible to lay these expressions aside seeing they are the words of God and not of man. The sermon is divided into two parts: 1) In what sense Christians are not perfect and 2) In what sense they are perfect.

---

[1]. Letter of 15th September, 1790, L. VIII, p. 238.

Wesley identified 'areas' in which Christians are not perfect. They are not perfect in knowledge and they are not so perfect in this life as to be free from ignorance. They may know things relating to this world, and with the world to come, and they may well know the general truths which God has revealed. They know in every circumstance of life what Christ requires of them and how to keep a conscious void of offence towards God and man. Yet they cannot search God out to perfection and no one is so perfect in this life as to be free from ignorance. As a consequence of this no one is free from mistake. It is true, says Wesley, that in the essential things to salvation a Christian does not make a mistake, but he does in the unessential i.e., with regard to facts. As regard to Holy Scripture even the best Christians are liable to mistake. Christians are also not so perfect as to be free from infirmities. Wesley means here not bodily infirmities but all those inward or outward imperfections which are not of a moral nature. Such are the weakness or slowness of understanding, dullness or confusion of apprehension, incoherency of thought, irregular quickness or heaviness of imagination. These are the infirmities which are found in the best of men in a larger or smaller proportion and from these none can hope to be perfectly freed, till the spirit returns to God that gave it. Man cannot be totally free from temptation as Christ was tempted even to the end of His Life.

Therefore Christian perfection does not imply an exemption either from ignorance, mistake, infirmities or temptations. It is only another term for holiness. They are two names for the same thing. There is no perfection of degress, none which does not admit of a continual increase. 'So that how much soever any man has attained, or in how high a degree soever he is perfect, he hath still need to 'grow in grace' and daily to advance in the knowledge and love of God his Saviour.'[1]

Wesley then turns his attention to describing in what sense Christians may be perfect. Christians who have been justified are made free from outward sin. This ceasing from sin, if it is interpreted in the lowest sense as regarding only the outward behaviour, must denote the ceasing from the outward act, from any transgression of the law. That salvation from sin was not given until Jesus was glorified is, Wesley says, testified by St. Peter when speaking of his fellows in the flesh, as now 'receiving the end of their faith, the salvation of their souls'.[2] Wesley appeals, among others, to St. John for support and claims that John declares; first, the blood of Jesus cleanses us from all sin; second, no man can say I have not sinned or I have no sin to be cleansed from; third, God is ready both to forgive our past sins and to save us from them for the time to come and fourth, that we need not continue in sin as we have an advocate with the Father, Jesus Christ the righteous. Therefore Wesley says a Christian is so far perfect as not to commit sin. Only of those, says Wesley who have overcome the wicked one, can it be said they are in such a sense perfect.

Christians are free from evil or sinful thoughts. Yet, thoughts concerning evil are not always evil thoughts, that a

---

1. Sermon on Christian Perfection, Forty Four Sermons, p. 462.
2. 1 Peter 1 vv 9 and 10.

thought concerning sin and a sinful thought are widely different. A man for instance may think of a murder which another has committed yet this is no evil or sinful thought. St. Mark says that it is out of the heart of man that evil thoughts proceed[1] but if the heart be no longer evil then evil thoughts can no longer proceed out of it. If the tree were corrupt so would be the fruit but the tree is good and the fruit is good.

As Christians are freed from evil thoughts so are they free from evil tempers. This, Wesley claims, is evident from Christ's declaration that the disciple is not above his Master but everyone that is perfect shall be as his Master. The Master was free from all sinful tempers so therefore is his disciple and every real Christian. As John says,[2] 'everyone that has Christ, the hope of glory in him, purifies himself even as He is pure.' He is purified from pride, for Christ was lowly of heart. He is pure from self-will or desire, for Christ desired only to do the will of His Father. He is pure from anger for Christ was meek and gentle, patient and long-suffering. Christ was angry at peoples' sin and yet at the same time grieved for the sinners - angry or displeased at the offence but sorry for the offenders. Christ, says Wesley, saves people from their sins, and not only from outward sins but also from the sins of their hearts, from evil thoughts and from evil tempers. Wesley claims with St. John that in this world our love is made perfect. This he also sees as the teaching of the first chapter of Philippines, 'God is light and in Him is no darkness at all. If we walk in the light . . .

[1]. Mark VII v 21.
[2]. l John III v 3.

we have fellowship one with another and the blood of Jesus Christ His Son cleanseth us from all sin.'[1]

The Apostle, says Wesley, is speaking of a deliverance in this world. If the cleansing here spoken of is no other than the cleansing us from the guilt of sin, then we are not cleansed from guilt, that is we are not justified unless we walk in the light as He is in the light. It remains, claims Wesley, that Christians are saved in this world from all unrighteousness; that they are now in such a sense perfect as not to commit sin, and to be freed from evil thoughts and evil tempers.

(ii)   A plain Account of Christian Perfection[2]

In this account Wesley describes the influences upon him which led him to take seriously the idea of perfection. In 1725 he read Bishop Taylor's 'Rules and exercises of Holy Living and Dying' and was affected especially by the part that relates to purity of intention. Instantly he resolved to dedicate his life to God in all his thoughts, words and actions. In 1726 he read Thomas à Kempis's book Christians Pattern from which Wesley said that the religion of the heart appeared in a stronger light than ever it had done before. The reading of Law's 'Christian Perfection' and 'Serious Call' a few years later, convinced Wesley of the absolute impossibility of being half a Christian and he determined to be all devoted to God.

1. Philippines 1 v 5.
2. Works XI, p. 366.

In 1733 Wesley preached at St. Mary's Church on the 'Circumcision of the Heart.' His conclusion gives us an insight into his doctrine on perfection.

> 'Here is the sum of the perfect law, the
> circumcision of the heart. Let the spirit
> return to God that gave it, with the whole
> train of its affections, other sacrifices from us
> He would not, but the living sacrifice of the
> heart hath he chosen. Let it be continuously
> offered up to God through Christ in flames of
> holy love.'[1]

In August 1735 Wesley records a conversation with one Arvid Gradin in Germany and said that this was the first account he had ever heard of a definition of the full assurance of faith. He records Gradin's experience in the following words:

> 'Response in the blood of Christ, a firm
> confidence in God, and persuasion of his
> favour, the highest tranquility, serenity, and
> peace of mind, with a deliverance from every
> fleshly desire, and a cessation of all, even
> inward sins.'[2]

The first tract that Wesley wrote on the subject was published in 1739 entitled 'The Character of a Methodist'. In this he described a perfect Christian placing in front 'Not as though I had already attained.' He says that a Methodist is one who loves the Lord his God with all his heart, his soul and mind and that, perfect love having now cast out fear, he reigns evermore. The Christian is

---

[1]. Works XI, p. 368.
[2]. Works XI, p. 370.

anxiously careful for nothing having cast all his care on God who cares for him. He prays without ceasing and his heart is lifted up to God at all times and in all places. Loving God, he loves his neighbour as himself. He is pure in heart for love has purified his heart from envy, malice, wrath and every unkind temper. None can take from him what he desires, for he does not love the world nor anything of the world but all his desires are in the love of God. He is bent on not doing his own will but God's will. The Christian has a single eye, and because his eye is single his whole body is full of light - God reigns alone and all that is in the soul is holiness. The Christian is known by his fruits. He is not content to keep the commandments but has in all points a conscience void of offence towards God and towards all people. His obedience to God is in proportion to his love, the source from which it flows. He is intent upon loving God. He does everything to the glory of God whether it be the important tasks or the trivial - 'whether he sit in the house, or walk by the way, whether he puts on his apparel, or labour, or eat and drink.'[1] The important rule is to do all in the name of Christ, giving thanks to God. The Christian cannot lay up treasures upon earth, or speak evil of his neighbour nor utter an unkind word of anyone - for love is the dominating factor.

Wesley records how after a while there was some opposition to what he was saying about perfection. He was attacked for dishonouring Christ and for asserting that he saves to the uttermost and by maintaining that Christ will reign in a person's

---

[1]. Works XL, p. 373.

heart and subdue all things to himself. As Wesley therefore believed that his doctrine was misunderstood and consequently misrepresented he judged it necessary to explain it further in the preface of the 'Second volume of Hymns' published in 1741. He says that the salvation of our souls is no other than the image of God freshly stamped on our hearts. God cleanses all the thoughts of the hearts by the inspiration of the spirit. Having hope, people see God as he is and purify themselves even as he is pure and are holy as he has called them holy in all manner of conversation. Not, says Wesley, that they have already attained all that they shall attain, but where the spirit is, there is liberty. Liberty from the law of sin and death. Christ has made them free from the root of sin, bitterness and pride. They feel that God is to them all-in-all and they are nothing in his sight. They are freed from self-will as desiring nothing but the holy and perfect will of God. They are freed from evil thoughts and they are free from wanderings in prayer. They are in one sense freed from temptation, and at all times their souls are even and calm. Their hearts are steadfast and unmoveable. Whoever has a sure confidence in God that his sins are forgiven, he is a child of God.

Wesley says that he is not affirming that all this salvation is given at once. There is, he claims, an instantaneous, as well as a gradual, work of God in his people. But

> 'we do not know a single instance, in any
> place, of a person's receiving in one and the
> same moment, remission of sins, the abiding

witness of the spirit, and a new, a clean
heart.'[1]

How God works, Wesley says, is not known but the general
manner in which he works is known. A person must be
convinced that he is 'poor and naked'. He remembers his sins and
he deserves damnation but then the Lord answers the cry of the
person and shows that he has taken away his sins and brings
peace and joy.   Sorrow and pain are fled away and then a person
has peace with God through Christ. In this peace a person may
abide for some time until the old sins return and he is thrown
into confusion, feeling that he has been deceiving himself in
thinking his sins are forgiven. Yet, the Spirit comes upon him and
he is indeed meek, gentle and teachable and it is at this point that
he sees the ground of his heart. He sees the depth of pride, self-
will, and hell. Yet, God is mindful of him and gives him a single
eye and a pure heart. He stamps upon him his own image and
superscription.

Wesley comments that this preface is the strongest account
he has yet given of Christian perfection. The beliefs expressed
above are to be seen in part of one of the hymns in the volume:

> Lord I believe a rest remains
> To all They people known;
> A rest where pure enjoyment reigns,
> And Thou art loved alone!
>
> A rest where all our soul's desire
> Is fix'd on things above;
> Where doubt and pain and fear expire
> Constant by perfect love.

---

[1]. Works XI, p. 380.

> Safe in the way of life above
> Death, earth and hell are mine,
> We find when perfected in love,
> Our long sought paradise.
>
> Come Father, Son and Holy Ghost,
> And seal me Thine abode
> Let all I am in Thee be lost,
> Let all be lost in God.[1]

According to Wesley the dispute was at its height in 1742 and he speaks clearly about perfection in a short preface to another volume of hymns. In it he claims that prejudice against perfection arises from a misapprehension of its nature. Wesley contends that there is no perfection in this life which implies any dispensation from attending all the ordinances of God. There is, further, no perfection in this life as implies an entire deliverance, either from ignorance or mistake in things not essential to salvation, from manifold temptations or from informities or from ignorance of many things. A person is perfect whom God has sanctified throughout in body, soul and spirit and one who walks in light. That person can testify that 'I am crucified with Christ', and his soul is all love filled with kindness, meekness, gentleness and long-suffering. He now does the will of God. To be a perfect man is to be sanctified throughout and to have one's heart aflame with the love of God. 'O that both we, and all who seek the Lord Jesus in sincerity, may thus be made perfect in one.'[2] The hymns naturally support what Wesley has been saying in the preface as is seen in the following verse:

---

1. Works XI, p. 382.
2. Works XI, p. 384.

'Saviour from sin I wait to prove
That Jesus is They healing name
To love, when perfected in love
Whate'er I have, or can or am,
I stay me on They faithful word,
The servant shall be as his Lord.

Thy own peculiar servant claim,
For Thy own truth and mercy's sake,
Hallow in me Thy glorious name,
Me for Thine own this moment take,
And changes and thoroughly purify
Thine only may I live and die.'[1]

On June 25th, 1744 the First Methodist Conference was held with six Clergymen and the preachers present. The conference considered sanctification or perfection.

'Question: What is implied in being a perfect Christian?
Answer: The loving God with all our heart and mind and soul.

Question: Does this imply that all inward sin is taken away?
Answer: Undoubtedly, or how can we be said to be saved from uncleanness.'[2]

At the fourth Conference held in June 1747 a number were present who did not believe in the doctrine of perfection and so the subject was again discussed. The division was upon whether a person was sanctified in the article of death or before. Those who could not accept the doctrine argued that one is entirely sanctified at the point of death and that until then a believer daily grows in grace and comes nearer and nearer to perfection. In response to

---

1. Works XI, p. 385.
2. Works XI, p. 385.

this the Conference noted that the term sanctified is continually applied by St. Paul to all who were justified; that this term alone means saved from all sin; that it is not proper to use it in that sense without adding the word wholly, and that it is important to speak almost continually of the state of justification but also concerning entire sanctification. Scripture is quoted to support the belief that one is saved from all sin before the article of death.[1]

'He shall redeem Israel from all his sins' (Psalm 130 v 8) and

> 'As Christ loved the Church and gave himself
> up for her, that he might sanctify her, having
> cleansed her by the washing of water with the
> word, that he might present the Church to
> himself in splendour, without spirit or wrinkle
> or any such thing, that she might be holy and
> without blemish'.

Matthew 5 v 48 is quoted to support the argument, 'Be you perfect as your Father who is in heaven is perfect.'

The conference stated that this perfection is to be done before death and says that from the very nature of a command which is not given to the dead but to the living. St. Luke is also quoted to support this:

> 'He has raised up a love of salvation for us, to
> perform the mercy promised to our fathers . .
> . That we being delivered out of the hands of
> our enemies, should serve him without fear,
> in holiness and righteousness before him and
> all the days of our life.'
>   Luke 1 v 69ff

---

[1]. Works XI, p. 387.

St. John is cited as an example of a person who has attained this perfection in the scriptures,

> 'Herein is our love made perfect, that we may
> have boldness in the day of judgement,
> because, as he is, so are we in this world.'
> 1 John 4 v 17

Wesley claims that at the end of this 1747 Conference there were no dissenting voices and all agreed. In 1749 Charles Wesley published 'Hymns and Sacred poems' and in these we see that John and Charles agreed on the idea of perfection. It is reflected in the following verses:

> Partner of Thy perfect nature,
> Let me be now in thee
> A new, sinless creature.

and

> Come in the accepted hour
> Bring Thy heavenly kingdom in!
> Fill us with the glorious power,
> Rooting out the seeds of sin.[1]

John and Charles Wesley maintained that Christian perfection is that love of God and our neighbour which implies deliverance from all sin; that is received merely by faith, that it is given instantaneously, in one moment; that it is to be expected not at death, but every moment that now is the accepted time, now is the day of salvation.

---

1. Works XI, p. 392.

At the Conference in 1759, John Wesley believed that there would be some who were unclear as to the doctrine of perfection which led him to publish 'Thoughts on Christian Perfection'. It begins with a definition of Perfection saying that all our thoughts, words and actions are governed by pure love. It is important that Christ is needed in every state and this is seen in that whatever grace man receives, it is a free gift from Him, that we receive it as his purchase, merely in consideration of the price he paid and that we have this grace, not only from Christ, but in him.

> 'For our perfection is not like that of a tree
> which flourishes by the sap derived from its
> own root, but like that of a branch which
> united to the vine bears fruit, but severed
> from it, is dried up and withered.'[1]

Wesley dwells on the belief that although one is perfected in love, it does not rule out mistakes - Love itself may induce one to make a mistake. Man cannot know infallibly that he is saved but there would be sufficient proof if the person behaved in an exemplory fashion and if he could give a distinct account of the time and manner in which he was changed and if it appeared that all his subsequent words and actions were holy and unblameable.

A question is raised as to what sort of children would be born to two perfect Christians. To answer this Wesley illustrates from gardening: 'Grafts on a crab-stock bear excellent fruit, but sow the kernels of this fruit and what will be the event? They produce as mere crabs as ever were eaten.'[2]   Wesley is insistent

---

1. Works XI, p. 396.
2. Works XI, p. 400.

that the meaning of perfection is to be based upon scripture. Scriptural perfection is pure love filling the heart and governing all the words and actions. The temptation is for the individual person to add ingredients of his own and to use his imagination and thus stray from the idea of scriptural perfection - of pure love reigning alone in the heart and life. He says that those who claim to have attained perfection should be examined with tenderness and without any harshness, sternness or sourness. It is extremely wrong, says Wesley, to rejoice as if one had found great spoils over someone who fails the test. Surely one should grieve and be deeply concerned . In 1762 Wesley records that many people who had cared for nothing religious were redeemed and that a considerable number of people believed that God had saved them from all sin. When Wesley left London where these things had taken place, enthusiasm had taken over and some began to take their own imaginations for impressions from God and to suppose that they should never die. They also believed they could not be tempted or feel pain and that they had the gift of prophecy and of discerning spirits. Wesley's reaction was to return to London to reprove them.

Wesley includes in his writing a letter written by Jane Cooper whom he describes as a living witness of Christian perfections. This is how the letter describes the change in her soul:

> 'From the time you preached (i.e. Wesley) on
> Galatians 5 v 7 I saw clearly the true state of
> my soul. That sermon described my heart
> and what it wanted to be, namely truly

happy. From that time the prize appeared in
view and I was enabled to follow hard after it.
I was kept watching into prayer, sometimes in
much distress, at other times in patient
expectation of the blessing.

I never knew as did then the force of these
words, 'be still and know that I am God'. I
became nothing before Him and enjoyed
perfect calmness in my soul. I promised if he
would save me from sin I would praise Him.
But I found these pleas to be nothing worth
and that if He saved me it must be freely for
his own name's sake.

I was in a moment enabled to lay hold on
Jesus Christ and found salvation by simple
faith. He assured me the Lord, the King was
in the midst of me and that I should see evil
no more. I saw Jesus altogether lowly, and
knew he was mine in all his offices. I feel no
pride nor any affection but what is placed on
Him I desire to be lost in that love which
passes knowledge.'[1]

In 1762 Wesley published 'Farther Thoughts on Christian
Perfection' as the number of those who believed they were saved
from sin were increasing. After reviewing some of the thoughts
already covered in 'Thoughts on Christian Perfection' Wesley gives
advice to those who are hindered from seeking faith and holiness
by the false zeal of others.

'The first advice is that they should watch and
pray continuously. If God has cast out sin,
they should see that it enters no more. It is
fully as dangerous as desire. it is easy to slide
back into it unawares, especially if one thinks
there is no danger in it. It is pride not only to
ascribe anything we have to ourselves but to

---

[1]. Works XI, p. 411.

think we have what we really have not. To imagine none can teach one but those who are themselves saved from sin is a great mistake. Be always ready to own any fault you have done. If you have at any time thought, spoke or acted wrong, be not backward to acknowledge it.

The second advice is to beware of the daughter of pride, enthusiasm. Give no place to a heated imagination and do not easily suppose dreams, voice, impressions, visions or revelations to be from God. They may be from him but they may be from nature. One general inlet to enthusiasm, is expecting the end without the means, the expecting knowledge without searching the scriptures, the expecting spiritual strength without constant prayer and steady watchfulness. The very desire of growing in grace may sometimes be an inlet of enthusiasm. As it continually leads us to seek new grace, it may lead us unawares to seek something else new besides new degrees of love to God and man. So it has led some to seek and fancy they had received gifts of a new kind such as:- being dead to all works and not being liable to death, pain or grief. A ground of these mistakes is not considering deeply that love is the highest gift of God - that all visions, revelations, manifestations are little things compared to love.

The third advice is to beware of Antinomianism - making void the law through faith. Enthusiasm leads to this. Beward of thinking, because I am filled with love, I need not have so much holiness, because I pray always, therefore I need not set time for private prayer, because I watch always. Therefore I have not set time for private prayer.'[1]

---

[1]. Works XI, p. 431.

The fourth advice is to beware of sins of omission and Wesley calls his people to leave no opportunity to doing good in any kind. Be zealous of good works, willingly omit no work, either of pity or mercy and be slow to speak and wary of speaking.

The fifth advice is to beware of desiring anything but God. 'Keep yourself pure and let your eye remain single and your body shall be full of light.'[1] Wesley calls people not to desire pleasing food, anything good or beautiful, money, praise or esteem. Only aim at pleasing God, whether by doing or by suffering.

The sixth advice is to beware of schism, of making a rent in the Church. The inward disunion, the members ceasing to have a reciprocal love one for another is the very root of all contention and every outward separation. If people are to avoid schism it is important, according to Wesley, for them to observe the rules of the Society and of the Bands. He calls his people not to condemn or think hard of those who cannot see just as they can, for this may easily lead to disunion. Wesley obviously believed in the fellowship of the Church.

The last advice is a call for the people to be exemplary in all things - in outward things, in little things and in the depth of seriousness. This advice is then enforced in a number of reflections which Wesley commends to his people. He says that the sea is an excellent figure of the fullness of God for as the rivers all return into the sea, so the bodies and souls return to

---

1. Works XI, p. 432.

God. The readiest way which God takes to draw a person to himself is to afflict him in that he loves most and to cause this affliction to arise from some good action done with a single eye, because nothing can more clearly show him the emptiness of what is most lovely and desirable in the world. True resignation consists in a thorough conformity to the whole will of God.

> 'To abandon all, to strip one's self of all, in
> order to seek and to follow Jesus Christ naked
> to Bethlehem, where he was born, naked to
> the Hall where he was scourged, and naked to
> Calvary, where he died on the cross, is so
> great a mercy, that neither the thing nor the
> knowledge of it is given to any, but through
> faith in the Son of God.'[1]

Wesley stresses the need for humility saying that true humility is a kind of self-annihilation and that is the centre of all virtues. Another reflection is that the bearing of suffering in meekness and silence is the sum of a Christian life. God is the first object of our love and it is important to exercise our love towards those who most shock the way we think. Wesley observes that prayer is very important and all is prayer when done in simplicity according to the order to God. In souls filled with love the desire to please God is a continual prayer. The soul must be dependent upon God. It is important to watch incessantly and in order to do this Wesley suggests that from time to time each soul should examine himself, for nothing tends to the full assurance of faith except through humility and the exercise of all good works.

---

[1]. Works XI, p. 437.

Charity cannot be practised right unless the soul exercises it the moment God gives the occasion and then retires the instant after to offer it to God by humble thanksgiving. This is to avoid the temptation which springs from the very goodness of these works and to unite the soul to God. Good works do not receive their last perfection until they love themselves in God. Fire is the symbol of love said Wesley and the love of God is the principle and the end of all our good works. The fire of divine love has the advantage over material fire in that it can re-ascend to its source and raise with it all the good works which it produces. By this means it prevents their being corrupted by pride, vanity or any evil mixture.

In 1764 Wesley wrote down in short propositions what he believed about Christian perfection.

'1.	There is such a thing as perfection, for it is again and again mentioned in Scripture.

2.	It is not so early as justification, for justified persons are to go on unto perfection. (Hebrews VI v 1)

3.	It is not so late as death, for Paul speaks of living men that were perfect. (Philippians 3 v 15)

4.	It is not absolute. Absolute perfection belongs not to man, not to angels but to God alone.

5.	It does not make a man infallible. None is infallible while he remains in the body.

6. It is sinless? It is not worth while to contend for a term. It is salvation from sin.

7. It is perfect love. (1 John 4 v 18) This is the essence of it, its properties, or inseparable fruits, are reigning evermore, praying without ceasing and in everything giving thanks.

8. It is improvable. It is far from lying in that indivisible point, from being incapable of increase, that one perfected in love may grow in grace far swifter than he did before.

9. It is amissible - capable of being lost.

10. It is constantly both preceded and followed by a gradual work.

11. But is it in itself instantaneous or not? An instantaneous change has been wrought in some beliefs but in some this change was not instantaneous.[1]

Wesley calls his people to take seriously this doctrine of perfection and to look at it from outside. In one view it is purity of intention, dedicating all the life to God. It is the devoting of all the soul, body and substance to God. In another view it is all the mind which was in Christ enabling souls to walk as Christ walked. It is the circumcision of the heart from our fullness. It is a renewal of the heart in the whole image of God. In another view it is the loving God with our heart, and our neighbour as ourselves.

---

[1]. Works XI, p. 441.

'Take it in which of these views you please (for there is no material difference) and this is the whole and sole perfection.'[1]

Having outlined Wesley's ideas of perfection we now turn to look at a number of important details.

(b) Christian perfection and practical mysticism

It was in 1725 that Wesley first became pre-occupied with Christian perfection which was due to being influenced by practical mysticism at Oxford. Christian perfection became an essential theme in Wesley, as in practical mysticism. This perfection was not confined to any particular class or group of people but is applied to all. This idea is to be found in Law.[2] As in practical mysticism this perfection was conceived as an inherent ethical change in a person and the Christian Life represented as a progressive development towards it. This idea is apparent in Francois de Sales when he was writing for the wives of noblemen.[3]

The purpose of religion was to bring about such perfection. Wesley agreed with the mystics that everything was directed towards a change which would qualify man for glorification. His ideas of perfection after his conversion experience in 1738 were in most reports identical with those before. Above all it is seen in love to God and our neighbour, the love of a whole and undivided heart. This would lend weight to the idea that the experience of

[1]. Works XI, p. 444.
[2]. Law 'Perfection' - W.2 111, p. 55f.
[3]. de Sales, Introduction to the devout life, p. 14.

1738 was not an evangelical but a mystical conversion - that is the conversion of a religious man to a higher state of religious devotion. As Piette says of Wesley's experience, it was 'sa conversion a l'amour de Dieu.'[1] As a result of this experience the feeling of intimate fellowship had definitely become the dynamic force in his inward life and the source of his strength.

In Wesley's description of perfection is to be seen the reflections of the view which appears in à Kempis, Taylor and Law. Tendencies typical of the catholic tradition in Taylor and Law, especially in the ideal of 'Imitatie Christi' and the idea of intention, are found in Wesley. To Wesley perfection was given the primary meaning of purity of intention, the imitation of Christ and the love of God and our neighbour. In the 'Character of a Methodist', as we have seen, purity of intention is the mark of perfection. The eye of the perfect man is turn to God alone whom he loves. To imitate Christ is also defined as perfection. This meant possessing the temper of Christ and living as he lived, with inward and outward conformity with the will of God. The hallmark of perfection as has been seen is perfect love which implies that no wrong temper, none contrary to love, remains in the soul and that all the thoughts, words and actions are governed by pure love. This love is accompanied by a pure heart.

The affinity to mysticism is apparent in the 'Plain account of Christian Perfection' which has been examined. From this purity of intention, the imitation of Christ and whole-hearted love of God

---

1. Piette, La reaction Wesleyenne dans l'evolution protestante, p. 443.

and our neighbour are specified as the factors determining perfection. In his sermon on 'Our Perfection' it is defined in this way: it means to love God with all one's heart and one's neighbour as oneself; the mind that is in Christ, the image of God, a recovery of man to the moral image of God; inward and outward righteousness; man's own perfect consecration to God; salvation from all sin.[1] Thus it is to be seen that there is close affinity between Wesley and practical mysticism yet his doctrine of perfection was not identical with that of practical mysticism and the experience of 1738 did make some differences.

Perfection for Law was a goal for human effort and was an unattainable ideal. The perfection was a gradual development in sanctification. Fundamental to his idea of Perfection was the inward piety of heart and mind and the Christian life was one of moral effort and self-denial.

Wesley was in full agreement with this attitude - perfection was the goal of man's effort but could not be realised in this life. Yet after his experience in 1738 perfection came to be regarded as something that could and should be realised in this life. It is considered to be a gift of God and the work of the Holy Spirit. Man was justified by faith and by faith he would be fully sanctified too. It was also seen to be instantaneous as perfection is seen as a work of God bestowed on man through sanctifying faith. Wesley is in harmony with practical mysticism in the sense that sanctification is a gradual process but he diverges from it in

---

[1]. Works VI, p. 431ff.

his doctrine of perfection. Wesley made entire sanctification one of the stages in the process of the Christian life. It became a higher stage after new birth. New birth which took place instantaneously was followed by a gradual sanctification preceding the instantaneous event of entire sanctification. Man could not expect entire sanctification unless he had already undergone the previous work of sanctification. In the work of perfection man was not altogether passive for it meant a total consecration of surrender by man of this whole heart to God. Wesley's view of perfection was an obtainable and higher stage in the Christian life after forgiveness and new birth. Luther believed that forgiveness, which at the same time meant the transformation of man, was in itself the highest expression of the Christian life. He saw the ethical change of man's will as an incomplete beginning. The Reformers believed that perfection was perfection in faith but Wesley believed it was an inherent ethical perfection in love and obedience. Calvin[1] and Luther[2] thought that inherent ethical perfection came only with death whilst Wesley believed that entire sanctification could be realised during life on earth.

---

[1]. F. Wendel Calvin, Sanctification can be no more than begun during this life, p.257.

[2]. E. Ebeling Luther, The Whole life of the people commits only of longing, seeking and praying . . . to be justified right up to the moment of death.', p. 163.

(c)   The difference between the new birth and perfect
      sanctification

The new birth and perfect sanctification are conferred on
man through faith.   The process of sanctification after new birth is
comparable to the development of natural life and this
development is due to faith.   When a person grows in faith he
grows equally in sanctity, love, humility and meekness.   The
essence of perfection and the goal of faith are love and the
Christian life is a development in love.   Perfection comes to mean
perfection in love.   In the new birth love has already been
instilled into the heart of man and from then on there is a gradual
development.   It seems that the distinction between new birth
and entire sanctification is nothing more than a difference in
degree in a continuous development.   As perfection is perfect love
it is therefore clear that this love must be of the same kind as that
granted to man at new birth.   The situation is clarified in the
Sermon on Patience where Wesley writes,

> 'It (entire sanctification) does not imply any
> new kind of holiness: Let no man imagine this.
> From the moment we are justified till we give
> up our spirits to God, love is the fulfillings of
> the law, of the whole evangelical law which
> took place at the Adamic Law, when the first
> promise of the seed of the woman was made.
> Love is the sum of Christian sanctification, it is
> the one kind of holiness, which is found only
> in various degree in believers who are
> distinguished by St. John into little children,
> young men and fathers.   The difference
> between them properly lies in the degree of
> love.'[1]

---

[1]. Sermon on Patience, 1788, Works VI, p. 488.

From this it is to be seen that the kind of life is the same in entire sanctification as in the new birth.

However, where perfection is identified as liberation from sin it is seen as a higher and different stage from that of the new birth. In the minutes of 1744 perfection involves a love incompatible with sin. The difference is further seen when deliverance from sin in perfect sanctification is regarded as analogous with the entrance of death into the body. This deliverance from sin is the death of sin.[1] Therefore it seems that perfection brings full deliverance from sin whereas in new birth the deliverance is only partial. The regenerate man was delivered from sin in the sense that he was non longer dominated by it. At this stage man can be said not to commit outward sin yet inward sin still remained. The root of sin still remained. Sin was still inherent in his heart and the regenerate man was still to some extent carnal. Perfection is seen as full deliverance from sin. As has already been noted the perfect change implies 'the circumcision of the heart from all filthiness, all inward as well as outward pollution,'[2] involving a total death to sin and an entire renewal in the love and image of God.

For Wesley perfection delivered man from the root of sin as the source of inward and outward sins. This meant that man was delivered from original sin. This is clarified in a sermon on 'The Repentance of Believers' where he writes:

---

1. Minutes, 1744, Works VIII.
2. A plain account, Works XI, p. 444.

'Indeed this is so evident a truth, that well
nigh all the children of God, scattered abroad,
however they differ in other points, yet
generally agree in this, of the body resist the
conquer both outward and inward sin:
although we may weaken our enemies day by
day, yet we cannot drive them out. By all the
grace which is given at justification, we cannot
extirpate them.   Though we watch and pray
ever so much we cannot wholly cleanse either
our hearts or hands.   Most sure we cannot, till
it shall please our Lord to speak to our hearts
again, to speak the second time, be clean and
only the leprosy is cleansed.   Then only, the
evil root, the carnal mind is destroyed; and
inbred sin subsists no more.'[1]

Wesley taught that absolute perfection was not attainable in
this life. As has been seen in the account of perfection it was
subject to the limitations of human life. No one could escape
certain kinds of ignorance and mistakes. In other words Wesley
was being practical and the idea of perfection was adjusted to the
present circumstances of man. The idea of the law is also
adjusted. The law given to Adam in his innocence was a law of
works. It required obedience in every respect to the law of God-
especially to the love of God. It also required that this obedience
should be perfect in degree. The new law is the law of Christ and
this law to which man is now subject is that of faith. Christ
established a law of faith which means that it is only through faith
that man can be sanctified and glorified as well as justified. This
law of faith is fulfilled through love so Wesley called it the law of
love.

---

1. The Repentance of Believers, 1767, Sermon II, p. 390.

The definition of perfection as deliverance from sin is taken by Wesley to mean that the fully sanctified do not deliberately transgress the law of love. Perfection comes to mean perfect purity in intention, will and in action in so far as these are determined by the individual will. Because Perfection means deliverance from original sin as well as from actual sin, then perfection comes to mean total resignation of the will of man to the will of God. The self-will which remained in the soul is now utterly annihilated.

(d) Sanctification and Atonement

The idea of forgiveness will surely be overshadowed by that of sanctification which, as Christian perfection, is present in its most pronounced form. This is seen especially in thinking in terms of Wesley's relative and subjective conception of sin. Relative perfection is subjective and concerns the intention and will and absolute perfection is objective and independent of man's potentialities. This duality means that on the one hand he does not regard the defects of the fully sanctified as sin in the proper sense of the word. There can be no sin, he says, when love is the only principle of action. Yet these mistakes and defects can also be regarded as sins in the sense that they constitute deviation from the perfect law. Yet Wesley insists that the fully sanctified stand in need of the blood of the atonement because of their transgressions. Even the most perfect have continual need of the merits of Christ, even for their actual transgressions. Even the best of men 'need Christ as their Priest, their Atonement, their

Advocate with the Father; not only as the continuance of their every blessing depends on his death and intercession, but on account of their coming short of the law of love.'[1]

Wesley maintains both the possibility of perfection on the one hand and on the other its relative character and the continuous need of forgiveness on the part of the fully sanctified. Even the most sanctified of Christians must live on the basis of forgiveness. It is important to recognise that the Christian life can persist only through increasing contact with Christ. This applies equally to the fully sanctified.

> 'In every state we need Christ in the following respects:-
>
> 1) Whatever grace we receive, it is a free gift from him. 2) We receive it as his purchase, merely in consideration of the price he paid. 3) We have this grace, not only from Christ, but in him. Forour perfection is not like that of a tree, which flourishes by the sap derived from its own root, but as was said before, like that of a branch which united to the vine, bears fruit, but severed from it is dried up and withered. 4) All our blessings, temporal, spiritual and eternal, depend on his intercession for us, which is one branch of his priestly office whereof therefore, we have always equal need.'[2]

Never for a moment can sanctity be separated from Christ and His work. It is accorded to man solely because of Christ's merit and cannot therefore be considered a merit of man.

---

[1]. Further thoughts on Christian Perfection, 1703, Works XI, p. 417.
[2]. Minutes, 1758, Works XI, p.395f.

It becomes clear then, as well as conceiving perfection as something relative and subjective, that the Christian should strive for the objective absolute standard of Christ. This objective idea of perfection carries with it a corresponding idea of sin. This can be seen from an examination of Lindstrom's tabular view of perfection. He firmly distinguishes between the two kinds of perfection - Adamic perfection which applied to Adam before the Fall and Christian perfection which man can now attain.

Adamic Perfection	Christian Perfection
Based on the convenant of works man must fulfil the law of works.	Based on the covenant of grace man must fulfil the law of faith.
<u>Signifies</u> perfect obedience to every point in this law. This holiness must be perfect in degree and continue without intermission throughout the whole of life.	<u>Signifies</u> perfect obedience in so far as this is attainable in the present circumstances of man. It means perfect love. This holiness is a perfection of motive not of degree. It concerns man's will and intention.
This is a perfect fulfilment of the law and perfect deliverance from sin in the absolute and objective sense.	This is a perfect fulfilment of the law and perfect deliverance from sin in the relative and subjective sense.

The relation between Perfection and Atonement can be expressed as follows, varying in aspect according to the point of view from which perfection is regarded.

From the absolute and objective standpoint	From the relative and subjective standpoint
He who is fully sanctified is imperfect.	He who is fully sanctified is perfect.

This means the because of innumerable defects he must transgress the absolute law. In this sense he is not free from sin.

This means that he perfectly loves God as his neighbour and is perfectly free from sin properly so called.

For this reason he is not free from guilt.

For this reason he is also free from guilt.

In order that he may not suffer damnation for his sin and guilt, he is every moment dependant on merit and intercession of Christ.

Yet in order to remain perfect he is every moment dependant on the merit and intercession of Christ.[1]

(e)   General Signs of Perfection

i)   Assurance - as in justification assurance of perfection derives from the witness of the spirit and from the fruit of the spirit. Perfection is known by the witness and the fruit of the spirit. At perfection the spirit bears witness that sins are taken away. The fully sanctified might also learn that this perfection has been accorded to them through the fruits of the spirit.

ii)   Humility - Wesley stresses the importance of humility although the meaning of the term seems to vary according to the particular stage in the order of salvation at which the person finds himself. In the Sermon on the Mount humility before justification means conviction of sin and guilt. It is identified with the repentance that precedes justifying faith. In justification humility is achieved by a sense of total dependence on God and he will feel a tender humiliation before God for the sins in the heart. After justification humility means the same as repentance.

---

[1]. Lindstrom, Wesley and Sanctification.

Humility is regarded by Wesley as a fruit of love.

> 'Nothing humbles the soul so deeply as love.
> It casts out all high conceits, engendering
> pride, all arrogance and over-weaning, makes
> us little, and poor, and base, and vile in our
> own eyes. It abases us both before God and
> man, makes us willing to be the least of all the
> servants of all and teaches us to say, 'A mote
> in the sun beam is little, but I am infinitely
> less in the presence of God."[1]

Therefore if there is progress in sanctification, there must be progress in humility. The fully sanctified are also perfect in humility.

(iii) <u>Perfection of Character</u> - Perfection to Wesley also means the perfection of personality. Perfection is not just in acts but in the disposition which lies behind them, the soul with all its tempers. He calls the perfected 'patterns of strict holiness.'[2] Perfection means the perfected and harmonious personality and it is presented as a perfection of character. Christianity in general can be considered not only as a principle in the soul but also as 'a scheme or system of doctrine which describes the character.'[3]

f)   <u>Love</u>

Since love is for Wesley the means of defining perfection it is important to note what he understands by it. God's love is

---

[1]. Sermon on Charity, 1788, Works VIII, p. 48.
[2]. Further thoughts on Christian Perfection, 1703, Works XI, p. 424.
[3]. Letter to Rev. Middleton, 1749, Works X, p. 72.

atonement and justification aims at the establishment of the law of love in the human heart. The object of salvation is the restoration in man of the love of God. This is brought about by faith but faith is only the means and the cause of love. Love is described as having eternal duration whereas faith is transitory, something that applies only to man's life on earth. Man's fellowship with God in sanctification is seen primarily as a fellowship not of faith but of love. Wesley's idea of love differs from that of the practical mystics in that they stressed man's love whereas Wesley stressed God's love. As sanctification is regarded as a consequence of saving faith in atonement, so love to God and our neighbour is linked up with faith in atonement and assurance of forgiveness. Love is seen as the direct fruit of justifying faith. Love to God is shed in our hearts by the spirit. God's love to man shown in the atonement precedes man's love. We love God because he first loved us.

> 'How came you then to love him at first? Was
> it not because you knew that he loved you?
> Did you, could you, love God at all, till you
> found and saw that he was gracious, that he
> was merciful to you a sinner? Pardoning love
> is still at the root of all. he who was offended
> is now reconciled.'[1]

Faith in God and the conviction of Him love are pre-requisites of man's love to Him. It is only through this faith that the heart of man receives the love of God and that man is led to love other men.

---

1. Works VIII, p. 24.

God's love is the cause, man's love to God and his neighbour are the natural consequences. God's love in Christ is the source of man's love to God and his neighbour. St. John expresses what Wesley believes, that we can love God only because God first loved us. Therefore love comes from God to man. Love to God is shed abroad in man's heart by the spirit and it is seen as a fire descending on his heart, a divine fire of love, coming to man from above.[1] The idea of love instilled on new birth is determined by the object but this love grows and develops.

Christian love for Wesley is also bound up with the idea of law. Love for God and our neighbour is regarded as the fulfilment of the law of love. Love is the fulfilment of the law not by delivering us from it but by compelling us to observe it. The Christian does not obey the law in fear but rather in love. When a man loves God this love will compel him to love his neighbour. This obedience to God comes to be regarded as the fruit of the Spirit. For the Christian it is happiness to do the will of God. If man keeps the commandments of God, by which man shows his love of Christ, then this is regarded as a work of Christ in him.

Love becomes ordered love and it can be measured in size and degree and be marked by reason. Love is seen as regulated. After saying that the Christian loves all men, Wesley also says:

> 'And yet this universal benevolence does in
> no wise interfere with a peculiar regard for
> his relations, friends, and benefactors; a
> fervent love for his country, and the most

---

[1]. Sermon on the death of Rev. G. Whitefield, 1770, Sermons II, p. 526.

84

endeared affection to all men of integrity, of clear and generous virtue.'[1]

For Wesley, love to God has a parallel in love to the world. Love to God is a kind of affection which should be directed towards God. Love is a whole hearted attitude to God, a means to attain the end of perfect and final union with Him. Love to God is always the main principle yet it is accompanied by neighbourly love. Both have their common source in God's love to man. God's love to man is the first but indirect course of man's love to his neighbour. Man loves God because He loves him; further, because he loves God he loves his neighbour. Neighbourly love is regarded as a necessary fruit of love of God.

When Christians experience God's love to man this becomes the foundation of the unity among them. The fellowship or sharing of all Christians is based on love as the fruits of faith. The fellowship is based on brotherly love between all Christians, a love that overrides distinctions of doctrine, ritual or ecclesiastical organisation. In the sermon on the use of money it is to be seen that self-love and neighbourly love appear as forms of an ordered love grounded on love to God. Self-love, says Wesley, must not be regarded as a rival to the love of God. Like neighbourly love, self-love operates within the framework of love to God.

---

1. <u>Works X</u>, p. 68.

CHAPTER SIX

FINAL SALVATION

The key to final salvation is faith. The man who through faith is justified and receives present salvation achieves final salvation through continuing in faith. Wesley calls this continuance in faith, the condition of final salvation. In the 'Sermon on the Righteousness of Faith' he writes:

> 'By the righteousness which is of faith is meant, that condition of justification (and, on consequence, of present and final salvation, if we endure therein unto the end) which was given by God to fallen man, through the merits and mediation of His only begotten Son.'[1]

Through the merits of Christ all those who remain in faith to the end, that is active in love, will be saved. The emphasis is strongly upon love,

> 'endureth to the end in humble, gentle, patient love, he and he alone shall through the merits of Christ inherit the kingdom prepared from the foundation of the world.'[2]

The condition necessary for final salvation is faith active in love. This of course is the condition for sanctification and if the Christian continues in faith he will also develop in faith. Therefore we see that sanctification is very much a gradual process.

---

[1]. The Righteousness of Faith, 1746, Sermons 1, p. 136.
[2]. Sermon on Charity, 1788, Works VIII, p.57.

'From that time (i.e. new birth) salvation
gradually increases in the soul. For so is the
kingdom of God, as if a man should cast seed
into the ground, and it springeth up, first the
blade, then the ear, after that the full corn in
the ear.'[1]

The Christian must work in faith and if this is so he will feel
no anxiety at all, but he must seek perfect sanctification. Perfect
sanctification should be regarded as a promise to be fulfilled by
God in his own time. According to Wesley it is by way of promise:

'Q.8. In what manner should we preach entire
sanctification?
A. 'Scarce at all to those who are not pressing
forward. To those who are, always by way of
promise, always drawing, rather than driving.
Q.9. How should we wait for the fulfilling of
this promise?
A. In universal obedience; in keeping all the
commandments; in denying ourselves, and
taking up our cross daily. These are the
general means which God hath ordained for
our receiving his sanctifying grace. The
particular one, prayer, searching the
scriptures, communicating and fasting.
Christian joyfulness should not be damped by
pressing forward.
Q.17. Why may we not continue in the joy of
faith even till we are made perfect?
A. Why indeed! since holy grief does not
quench this joy; since even while we are
under the cross, while we deeply partake of
the suffering of Christ, we may rejoice with joy
unspeakable.
Q.18. Do we not discourage believers from
rejoicing evermore?
A. We ought not to so to do. Let them if
lightness or pride should mix with their joy, let
us not strike at the joy itself, (this is the gift of

---

[1]. A Farther Appeal, 1745, Works VIII, p.48.

God) but at that lightness, or pride, that the
evil may cease and the good remain.'[1]

'And if you thus taste of the good word and of
the powers of the world to come, you will not
murmur against God, because you are not yet
meet for the inheritance of the saint in light.
Instead of repining at your not being wholly
delivered, you will praise God for us for
delivering you. You will magnify God for what
he hath done, and take it as an earnest of what
He will do. You will not fret against Him,
because you are not yet renewed, but bless
Him because you shall be, and because now is
your salvation from all sin nearer than when
you first believed. Instead of uselessly
tormenting yourself because the time is not
fully come, you will calmly and quietly wait
for it, knowing that it will come and will not
tarry. You may therefore the more cheerfully
endure, as yet, the burden of sin that still
remains in you, because it will not always
remain. Yet a little while and it shall be clean
gone.'[2]

The Christian who lives in faith can look forward in
confidence to the glory which will be revealed. Wesley is careful
to present evangelically the perfection which is a necessary
condition for entry into eternal life. In a letter to Elizabeth Hardy
he describes this perfection:

'By perfection I mean perfect love, or the
loving God with all our heart so as to rejoice
evermore, to pray without ceasing and in
everything to give thanks. I am convinced
that every believer may attain this; yet I do
not say he is in a state of damnation or under
the curse of God till he does attain. No, he is

1. Works VIII, p.298.
2. Satan's devices, Sermon II, p.203.

in a state of grace and in favour with God as long as he believes.'[1]

Continuing faith stands out as the fundamental and ultimate condition of final salvation. It results sooner or later in perfect sanctification. Although salvation is by faith Wesley lays stress on works. The importance of works in the development of the Christian life is expressed. In 1744 Question 11 at the Conference was 'Are works necessary to the continuance of faith? Answer: Without doubt for a man may forfeit the free gift of God either by sin of omission or commission'.[2] The Christian life according to Wesley is marked by human activity. If it is to be upheld and developed, God's faithful care for those he has called must be accompanied by their obedience.

The importance of works is clearly shown when they are called a condition for final justification or when perfect sanctification is regarded as necessary to final salvation. The works issuing from faith are not regarded as pre-requisites of a second and final salvation, they are only the necessary fruits of true faith. When considering final salvation, works take a further significance. Final justification is considered dependent upon them. This is made clear in a 'Farther Appeal' Speaking of final salvation, Wesley calls holiness or universal obedience the ordinary condition. Faith is the only condition for present salvation but for final salvation works are also necessary.

> 'With regard to the condition of salvation it
> may be remembered that I allow, not only
> faith, but likewise holiness or universal

1. Letter to Elizabeth Hardy, April 1758, Letters LV, p.10.
2. Minutes, 1745, Works VIII, p.283.

> obedience, to be the ordinary condition of
> final salvation; and that when I say, Faith
> alone is the condition of present salvation,
> what I would assert is this; 1) that without
> faith no man can be saved from his sins; can
> be either inwardly or outwardly holy. And 2)
> that at what time soever faith is given,
> holiness commences in the soul. For that
> instant 'The love of God' (which is the source
> of holiness) is shed abroad in the heart.'[1]

Thus man's relation to God is seen by Wesley in terms of works as well as grace. Works are said to constitute a necessary condition for final salvation in the arguments against Antinomianism. Wesley writes,

> 'Labour, literally, work, for the meat that
> endureth to everlasting life. And in fact every
> believer, till he comes to glory works for as
> well as from life. Final salvation presupposes
> works as a condition.'[2]

Thus it is seen that the obedience and works issuing from faith can be directly or indirectly called necessary conditions of final justification. When Wesley says that at the last judgement man will be justified because of his works, no merit is involved in the concept of works. Justification is occasioned by the merits of the life and death of Christ. It is the witness, not the merit, of works that Wesley has in mind when he makes final justification dependent upon them.

---

1. A Farther Appeal Works VIII, p.68f   A Farther Appeal, Works VIII,
2. Works VIII, p.337.

Also necessary to final salvation is obedience and holiness.
Yet in final as well as present salvation everything is dependent
upon Christin's work of atonement. The idea of grace is also seen
in the fact that the works necessary to final salvation are regarded
as having been made possible by God. The grace of salvation is in
Wesley the common foundation of all the phases in the process of
salvation. Present salvation related to faith and final justification
is related to the fruits of faith. The importance Wesley attributes
to works is chiefly grounded on his objection to the Calvinist
doctrine of election.[1] No one, Wesley claims, can be lost except as
a result of his own actions. Faith is the condition of salvation just
as absence of faith is the condition of damnation. Faith is a
personal act on the part of man and of independent importance
for salvation. A Christian is already saved in faith but at the same
time he is ceaselessly exhorted to continue in faith by means of
obedience and to seek the sanctity which constitutes the pre-
requisite of final salvation.

Yet, works are subordinate to grace for the initiation always
rests with God and at every stage of the order of salvation the
effective course is always God's grace.

---

1. F. Wendel, Calvin. p.263ff.

CHAPTER SEVEN

CONCLUSION

St. Francis de Sales, in the preface of his book Introduction to the Devout Life says 'It is true, dear reader, that here I write of a devout life without being devout myself. Yet it is certainly not without a desire of becoming so, and it is this affection for devotion that encourages me to instruct you.'[1] It may be assumed that John Wesley wrote on Christian perfection in the same spirit. He urged the call to holiness because to him it was one of the most important things in life, yet, like St. Paul, he never claimed that he, personally, had attained entire sanctification although he often asserted that a great many Methodists had received this gift. Wesley's great contribution to thinking concerning the spiritual life can best be appreciated if we view it from three perspectives. First, we need to consider the background and schema of the spiritual life which he sought. Secondly, we need to release his doctrine from its outmoded expression. Finally, by adopting some existentialist perspective we can appreciate the value of his own spiritual life.

(a) Wesley's schema of the spiritual life

Wesley was in no doubt as to where the Christian life begins. It begins in the Divine initiative: we love because he first loved us. In this way Wesley is just as orthodox and catholic as, say, St. Bernard of Clairvaux.[2] The gospel would not be good news if it were a summons to our search for God, to moral effort which

---

1. Francis de Sales, Introduction to the Devout Life, p.30.
2. St. Bernard, On the love of God, p.13.

Baker teaches in Sancta Sophia.[1] It is the offer of the love of God in Christ, which knows no respect of persons and is free for all who will accept it, however sinful they may be. This makes Wesley a Protestant evangelical, (Arminian, not Calvinist) that is one who believed that grace was not irresistible and man was at liberty to reject God's offer. But his spiritual theology was based on love of God rather than faith in Christ. Love of God mean's God's love, not ours which is not worth considering. Yet love always want to create the response of love in the beloved. If we are to love God in return we must keep his law which is to love him with our whole being and our neighbour as ourselves. This meant a disciplined 'methodist' life.

Wesley was even more interested in what happened after conversion to Christ than in conversion itself. The convert is but a body in Christ and he must not be left without nurture or given a perpetual diet of milk. He must be encouraged to attain nothing less than the measure of the stature of the fullness of Christ.

Wesley's map of the spiritual progress was never as refined as St. John of the Cross despite some similarities of thought. It would be useful nonetheless to compare Wesley's map of spiritual progress with that of St. John of the Cross. Broadly speaking St. John's stages of progress were as follows:

'Purgative way	(Beginners
	(Active night of the senses
Transition	Passive night of the senses
Illuminative way	(Quiet) Active night of the spirit
Transition	Passive night of the spirit

---

[1]. A. Baker: Sancta Sophia. p.384ff.   'Of acts of the will and affections'.

Unitive way   Spiritual betrothal
                         Spiritual marriage'[1]

Wesley lays stress on the <u>examination</u> of the state of our
souls, 'It is good to renew ourselves from time to time, by closely
examining the state of our souls, as if we had never done it
before.'[2]   Examination, we recall, was part of the 'ritual'
recommended by Peter of Alcantara and used by St. John for the
beginners in prayer. Wesley emphasised doing the <u>will of God.</u>
'True resignation consists in a thorough conformity to the whole
will of God.'[3] Wesley expresses this conformity in keeping the
moral law. Likewise St. John claims that for every Christian it
should be the chief aim of his life to conform to the expressed will
of God, that is to obey his commandments and precepts as he
understands them in order to apply them to the situations of
everyday life.

The virtue of <u>humility</u> is looked upon by Wesley as an
essential part of spiritual growth. 'Humility and patience are the
surest proofs of the increase of love. Humility alone unites
patience with love. True humility is a kind of self-annihilation
and this is the centre of all virtues.'[4] Humility is nothing other
than a sense of reality concerning ourselves, our fellow creatures
and our creator. True humility accepts that all other are better
than we ours elves and sees in them virtues which we ourselves
lack. St. Teresa of Avila believed that God offered no resistance to
perfect humility and St. John agreed with her.

---

1. E.W.T. Dicken, <u>Crucible of Love,</u> p.293.
2. <u>Works XI,</u> p.439.
3. <u>Works XI,</u> p.436.
4. <u>Works XI,</u> p.437.

Wesley's ideal was a very simple life-style and this is seen in his <u>Sermon on the Use of Money</u> where he encouraged his people 'to gain all you can, save all you can and give all you can.'[1] Yet it went deeper than this for underlying all this was his insistence upon detachment which is a godly indifference to any personal advantage or the satisfaction to be derived from the order of created things.   Detachment requires not that we shall have no possessions but we shall desire none.   Detachment is a detachment from all that is not God.   What is required for true detachment is not infliction upon oneself of pain and hardship but the observance of a rule.   St. John of the Cross sets it out in the Ascent

> Always choose
> not the easiest, but the most difficult
> not the most delectable, but the most insipid
> not the most pleasing, but the most displeasing
> not that which is most restful, but that which is most laborious
> not the greatest but the least
> not the highest and the most prized but the lowest
> not to desire anything but to desire nothing.'[2]

The words of the Methodist Covenant service, which Wesley first held in the French Church at Spitalfields on August 11 1755 echo St. John.

> 'I am not longer my own but Thine. Put me to
> what Thou wilt, rank me with whom Thou wilt,
> put me to doing, put me to suffering, let me be

---

1. <u>Sermons XLIV.</u>
2. John of the Cross, '<u>Ascent</u>'.

employed for Thee or laid aside for Thee,
exalted for Thee or brought low for Thee, let
me be full, let me be empty; let me have all
things, let me have nothing; I freely and
heartily yield all things to Thy pleasure and
disposal.'[1]

St. John and Wesley both valued the need to love God and our neighbour. Time and time again it is to be seen in Wesley's treatment of perfection which is defined as perfect love. Total sanctity involves total selflessness and self-sacrifice in favour of our fellow men. Equally important is that we bear no grudge and harbour no resentment against one another. Love which is to be aimed for is a love altogether free from self-regarding motives, a love which is spontaneous and devoid of all self-consciousness.

By stressing humility, detachment and love of God and neighbour and making them essential for growth in sanctification, Wesley, presumably without knowing it, was in harmony with the Carmelite Saints. St. Teresa spoke of those pre-requisites of true peace; 'The first is love of one another, the second detachment from all created things, the third is true humility, which although I speak of it last is the most important and embraces all three.'[2]

It would be wrong to force any further comparison between Wesley and the Carmelites but as has been seen the foundations are similar. It has been seen that the spiritual process in Wesley is seen as a gradual development and that the gradual process is interrupted by the direct intervention of God which in a single

1. Book of Offices, 1936, p.118.
2. St. Teresa, The Way of Perfection.

instant raises man to a higher plane. If preparations are included for the Christian life and its perfection after death, the process comprises the following stages: first repentance or conviction, justification including new birth, sanctification - in the sense of entire sanctification or Christian perfection - and glorification. Wesley took great pains to unify the divine factors in salvation. Forgiveness and new birth are obviously very closely related - the one cannot occur without the other. After new birth, sanctification develops towards the perfect real change that constitutes the pre-requisite of final salvation and glorification. There is a certain organic relationship between the separate phases of the process of salvation. Yet the idea of organic unity does not prevent Wesley from regarding forgiveness and new birth, or present and final salvation, as separate and distinct one from the other.

Forgiveness and sanctification are the two important factors in Wesley's idea of salvation with the main stress on sanctification. Forgiveness is based on atonement, which is the ground of the Christian life, yet it is the idea of sanctification - of growing in perfect love - that is the dominating factor. The idea of salvation is determined by the idea of perfection because salvation is seen as a process directed to the perfect, real change of the individual. This process is the necessary condition for final salvation. The Christian is above all a pilgrim, his life on earth is a journey and the destination is heaven.

The nerve of the doctrine of perfection is that the Christian must never be complacent about his progress in grace, and his behaviour and attitudes must not willingly go on in the same faults. He must set no limits to the victory of the divine love in him.

(b) A restatement

The term perfection for what Wesley had in mind is really the wrong word. Indeed in appears plain that he wanted to drop it himself.[1] It is a mystery that he made such free use of a name he did not like. He used it no doubt for the same reason that he used the name Methodist: because others used it and because it was the swiftest way to recognition. His better term was perfect love which, although it contains the word perfect which when used as an adjective and not a noun, is less aggressive. Perfect love is positive. The idea of perfection as sinlessness gave a picture of the ideal in terms of negation. It never really grappled with the sins of omission. It is also social, for holiness conceived as perfect love can never be a selfish cult. One of the demerits of the term Christian Perfection is that its ideal is static. Sinless ness is its keynote. Evil is cast out. Right at its heart there is holy egoism. Duty is the keystone. One of the hardest things to bear is the discovery that our passionate devotion to duty as the means to holiness may be a disguise for exhibitionism. Yet it is different when we enter the realm of supernatural love. Christian morality is not a list of things to be left undone. It is an active, vital principle. It touches other life on all sides. Wesley never tired of insisting that love was the mainspring of the holy life yet had he held to his title of perfect love certain defects in his doctrine would not have developed. For instance, Wesley's doctrine of sin

---

[1]. Letters III, p.167

is defective in its failure to deal with the sins of omission. If sin is a voluntary transgression of a known law, the sin is the positive thing and the holiness is nothing. The sins of omission have slipped through the net. No known law has been transgressed. Yet they remain a leprosy of the soul and fruitful of the most terrible penalty which can overtake mankind.[1] But holiness conceived as perfect love is utterly free of thius defect. Love has a keener vision than duty. The positivity of love is the answer to weakness. Hating oneself can become as obsessional as hating others. Not purgation and more purgation but love and more love for 'We are not saved by what we know but what we love.'[2]

The hardest and least defensible part of Wesley's doctrine is that of assurance. Why is it dangerous for even a devout soul conscious of nothing but supernatural love to say that he is free from sin? First, because the words which are being used has a limited meaning. Second, a claim of this tremendous character is hard to harmonise with a moment-by-moment life. It is questionable whether the statement is in any way unremarkable if it refers only to the moment of its utterance. Third, if the words 'free from sin' have any reference beyond the immediate moment, it is a witness shaped in ignorance because no person knows what is in him. Fourth, there is the awful danger of presumption and pride and the self-induced spiritual blindness, (this is a recurring phenomenon of this claim,) which should check every public utterance that all sin has gone. Instead of keeping the stress on love it seems that Wesley stressed sinlessness and almost made it

1. Hebrews, 2 v 3.
2. G. C. Cell, The Rediscovery of John Wesley, p.349.

a cardinal article of faith. The idea that one has already achieved perfection can become an impediment to spiritual progress. Sanctity and sin live together in the heart. However, Wesley did believe that sin could enter again into the fully sanctified heart and rob the most assured of their assurance.

Wesley's Journal, taken as a whole, suggests that the author had no interest in anything but souls. When we read it more carefully it is clear that he was not only interested in the soul but with the deeper, harder questions concerning the origin of needs and how social maladjustments might be overcome. The acquisition and use of wealth, the economic consequences of luxury, the shifting population from the country to the towns and the problem of unemployment, they all receive some comment from him. [1] Wesley was a practical person and his call to holiness was rooted in the culture of his day. It led to tension then as it does today if we take the call to holiness seriously. The numerous situations in which the conscience of an earnest Christian can be strained by the deceits of competitive business life today, but against which it is so perilous to protest if he is to live at all, are known to those who speak honestly. To say that it is impossible to live the Christian life in commerce is an exaggeration and sometimes it is just a defence mechanism against the accusation of an outraged and restive conscience. Yet is is clearly seen that the path to perfection is easily impeded. In the nature of things a compromise seems inevitable. If a Christian concludes that it is impossible to live a perfect life in an imperfect world he must not

---

[1]. Works, III, p. 271.

resent it if he is reminded that Christ did. Christ only lived a perfect life in the sense that he always acted with a perfect motive. He did not always do what a perfect man would do in a perfect world. In the latter there would have been no whip for the Temple traders, no woes for the Pharisees and no tribute money for the foreign conqueror. For the Christian seeking perfection today, the word sin takes on a wider connotation. It is seen in social guises: the selfishness which clings to dubious theories of economics, the jealousy which guards existing privileges and will not meet a challenge concerning their legitimacy and the wilful ignorance of the circumstances of other people's lives. These Christians find their consciences troubled as they see the absence of a really fair choice of rich Christian life for those who are haunted by continual unemployment and the vast inequalities of opportunity which exist in regard to health, education and leisure. Those who seek perfection can no longer find their definition of sin exhausted by lewd thoughts and drunkenness. Sin is also an evil social system. When sin is confessed, the need for forgiveness is not only individual but also for a failure to follow Christ in the redemption of social life. Not only is sin widened in meaning but also perfection. It becomes richer and does not concern itself only with private virtues. There is much for those who seek perfection to learn: patience with the slow development of those who have been underprivileged in the past, patience with those in whom it seems too hard to create any desire for nobler things and courage to face the subtler evasions of sin in their own souls and to overcome the temptation to return to the narrower concept of holiness because it is less costly and more comfortable.

In the light of Wesley's doctrine it is clear that many Christians live on a sub-Christian level. That is not a judgement made in spiritual pride nor a judgement which omits the critic himself. The Church is living far below the New Testament offer and promise. There is not enough difference between people outside the Church and people inside. Many cheerfully ignore the Christian faith, repudiate public worship, private prayer, and all the means of grace and believe that they live as good a life as their Church-attending neighbours. And in a good number of instances Christians lack a qualify of life. The Church, without belittling numerous societies for good, is disunited, enfeebled and in retreat in the western world. Amongst all this there is a need for holiness, with is potent. Like the word of God it is living and active. It rebukes sin. It creates the appetite for itself. It fosters faith. If we think of holiness in terms of the strong positive gift of perfect love it strains the imagination and brings new hope. No person is quite the same after contact with a saint.

Many Christians today lack any sense of goal. Confirmation is often seen as an end in itself. The Christian is not held by a vision of glory and few have a sense of the numinous. There is little to suggest that Christians know their goal and a good deal of uncertainty abounds. A clear conviction received into the mind that God is able and willing and eager to deal drastically with sin in us, the sins of the mind as well as the sins of the flesh, the jealousies, pettinesses, irritabilities, resentments, egotisms. The constant attending to God that one may receive this present salvation and know in experience the deep difference between a straining effort to do the thing oneself, and the bewildering awareness that God has done something Himself. Such a conviction and such an experience calls the Christian on and makes it obvious to all that he is a person progressing in Christian experience with a pre-view of his goal.

Although there has been some renewed interest in the doctrine of the Holy Spirit - mainly through the Charismatic movement - the doctrine is nonetheless neglected. The mass of Church people receive the doctrine of the Spirit's personality and His power as taught but their powerless lives remind one of the men at Ephesus whom Paul challenged with the words 'Did you receive the Holy Spirit when you believed?'[1] Wesley did not care to describe the gift of perfect love as the reception of the Holy Spirit because he held that the Holy Spirit was given when a man first believed and entire sanctification he regarded as a subsequent blessing. Yet the life and literature of early Methodism are full of doctrine of the Holy Spirit and that God the Spirit was peculiarly with sanctification is clear. Wesley says that it is the Holy Spirit which is responsible for:

> 'The conversion and entire sanctification of
> our hearts and lives. The title 'holy' applied
> to the spirit of God does not only denote that
> He is holy in His own nature, but that He
> makes us so; that He is the great fountain of
> holiness to His Church; the Spirit from where
> flows all the grace and virtue...'[2]

---

1. Acts. 19 v 2.
2. Works VIII, p. 485f.

103

Power was promised with the Holy Spirit[1] and the first.
fruit of the Spirit is love.[2] Christians today need power and
perfect love. On the promise of Christ, God is pledged to give the
Holy Spirit to those who ask Him.[3] He gives - for the Spirit is not
to be strained after. Only those who have strained after holiness
by their own effort will know the weariness and disappointment
of it. The Holy Spirit with the endowment of power against sin is
a supernatural gift. It is equally important to emphasise that
stress on the active principle of holiness as a gift does not cancel
out all discipline from the devotional life. Discipline is an integral
part of the holy life - not the toilsome, straining, failing effort to
be good - but the faithful attending on God to receive. The Faith
of one high moment cannot secure holiness for ever - it is a life of
intimate relationship which issues in mystic indwelling and
faithfulness shows itself in our consistency in attending. Wesley
was a man of iron discipline from his youth.. He was unshaken in
discipline and when illumination came he carried the discipline
over to be the servant of his enlightened mind. Most Christians
reverse Wesley's order. Enlightenment comes first and thus the
need to forge the discipline afterwards. Sometimes they cease to
wait upon God and this is a heavy price. There can be no real
continuance of the holy life in the soul of any person who does
not continuously wait on God. Nothing incites to holiness or
perfect love like the contemplation of it, but it must be
contemplation, not in abstract but in Christ and in the saints. This
is made clear in Wesley's description of Madeley:

---

1. Acts. 1 v 8.
2. Galations 5 v 2.
3. Luke II v 13.

'Within fourscore years I have known many
excellent men, holy in heart and life, but one
equal to him, I have not known, one so
uniformly and deeply devoted to God, so
unblameable a man, in every respect, I have
not found either in Europe or America. Nor do
I expect to find another such on this side of
eternity.'[1]

Thus this brief restatement of Wesley's doctrine of perfection leads us to conclude that it is no dead doctrine but one which, if brought alive, would inspire the individual Christian and the Church itself.

(c) Wesley - a spiritual man

It is important to realise that behind the proclamation of a doctrine such as that of Christian perfection there was a person who himself was travelling the road of sanctification. His holiness shines through his poems and hymns.

His spiritual life was based upon a rule of life on which he built his idea of perfect love. The rule was as follows:

1. Begin and end every day with God: and sleep not immoderately.
2. Be diligent in your calling.
3. Employ all spare hours in religion as able.
4. Keep holy-days.
5. Avoid drunkards and busybodies.
6. Avoid curiosity and all useless employments and knowledge.

---

[1]. Works XI, p.365.

7.   Examine yourself every night.

8.   Never on any account pass a day without setting aside at least an hour for devotion.

9.   Avoid all manner of passion.

William Law's influence on Wesley is here very evident. It was Law who taught him not only to read but to study the Bible and to apply it to himself, to make it his frame of reference for all the events, circumstances and discussions of his life.

The Eucharist was for Wesley supreme for it was a sign of God's free grace as well as having a societary aspect. At a time when the Church of England bishops were exhorting their clergy to interpose one celebration between Pentecost and Christmas, Wesley was receiving Communion every few days. In the Hymns on the Lord's Supper there is a high doctrine of Eucharistic sacrifice and an affirmation of the real presence, though with an agnosticism as to its manner.

> 'To every faithful soul appear
> and show They real presence here.'[1]

Wesley's spirituality was joy and peace in believing. He expected his people to enjoy their religion and the exercises in meditation he taught them would sometimes bring them to an ecstatic pause as they glimpsed something of the glories of the kingdom of God.

---

[1]. Hymns and Poems 629. C. Wesley.

The Christian Way is described by Wesley in this way.

> 'To abandon all, to strip one's self of all, in
> order to seek out and to follow Christ naked
> to Bethlehem, where he was born, naked to
> the hall where he was scourged, naked to
> Calvary where he died on the cross is so great
> a mercy, that neither the thing, nor the
> knowledge of it, is given to any, but through
> faith in the Son of God.'[1]

The Life of prayer is discussed:

> 'All that a Christian does, even in eating and
> sleeping is prayer, when it is done in
> simplicity, according to the order of God,
> without either adding to or diminishing from
> it by his own choice.'

> Prayer continues in the desire of the heart,
> though the understanding be employed in
> outward things.

> In souls filled with love, the desire to please God is a
> continued prayer.'[2]

Whatever else may be said of Wesley he was a person who taught and encouraged others to seek for perfect love. This is seen in a poem which he made his own translated from the German, and which sums up the whole of his life and teaching.

---

1. Works XI, p.435.
2. Works XI, p.435

'O grant that nothing in my soul
May dwell but Thy pure love alone
O may Thy love possess me whole
My joy, my treasure and my crown,
Strange flames far from my heart remove
My every act, word, thought, be love.[1]

Paulus Gerhardt (1606-76)

---

[1]. Poetic Works Vol.I, p.138

BIBLIOGRAPHY

Primary Sources

Wesley, J. The Works. Preface to the Third Edition 1831 by Thomas Jacksion, Editions I-XIV. London.

Wesley, J. Standard Sermons. Edited and Annotated by E. Sugden. I. The Second Edition, London, 1935. II. London, 1921.

Wesley, J. The Journal. Edited by Nehemiah Curnock. Standard Edition, I-VIII. London, 1909-1916.

Wesley, J. The Letters. Edited by J. Telford. Standard Edition, I-VIII. London, 1931.

Wesley, J. Explanatory Notes upon the New Testament. The Second Edition. London, 1757.

Wesley, J. 'A short view of the difference between the Moravian Brethren . . . . . and the Revd. Mr. John and Charles Wesley. Extracted chiefly from a late journal.' The Second Edition, Bristol, 1748.

Wesley, J. and Wesley, C. The Poetical Works. Collected and arranged by G. Osborn, I-XIII, London.

Wesley, C. Short Hymns on Select Passaged of Scriptures, 1762.

Wesley, C. Collection of Hymns for the use of the People called Methodists, 1780.

Secondary Sources

à Kempis, Thomas. Of the Imitation of Christ, London, 1885.

Baker, A. Sancta Sophia.

Bett, H. The Spirit of Methodism, London, 1937.

Bicknell, E. J. A Theological Introduction to the Thirty-nine Articles of the Church of England, London, 1919.

Book of Offices, 1936.

Cannon, W. R. The Theology of John Wesley.

Carter. H. The Methodist heritage.

Cell, G. C. The rediscovery of John Wesley. New York, 1935.

Davies, R. Methodism, Pelican, 1963.

De Sales, F. Introduction to the devout life translated by Michael Day. Dent & Sons, 1961.

Deschner, J. W. Wesley's Christology.

Dicken, E. W. T. The Crucible of Love.

Eayres, G. John Wesley, Christian Philosopher and Church Founder, London, 1926.

Ebeling, G. Luther. Collins, 1970.

Edwards, M. John Wesley and the 18th Century.

Edwards, M. Methodism and England. A study of Methodism in its social and political aspects during 1850-1932, London, 1943.

Flew, R.N. The idea of Perfection in Christian Theology, Oxford, 1934.

Forsyth, P. T. Christian Perfection.

Green, J.R. A short history of the English people.

Haddal, I. John Wesley. Epworth, 1961.

Hildebrandt, F. Christianity according to the Wesleys.

Inge. Studies of English Mystics, London, 1921.

Law, W. A practical treatise upon Christian Perfection, London, 1726.

Law, W. A serious call to the devout and holy life, London, 1906.

Law, W. The case of Reason, or Natural Religion, Fairly and Fully Stated, London, 1731.

Linstrom, H. Wesley and Sanctification, Epworth, 1961.

Longridge, W. H. The Spiritual Exercises of St. Ignatius Loyola, London, 1919.

Martin, D. The breaking of the Image. Blackwell, 1980.

Martin, D. A Sociology of English Religion, SCM, 1967.

Monk, R.C. Johnm Wesley: His puritan heritage.

Otto, R. The idea of the Holy.

Outler, A. C. John Wesley.

Overton. John Wesley.

Peters, John L. Christian Perfection and American Methodism.

Piette, M. John Wesley in the Evolution of Protestantism.

Pope, W.B. A compendium of Christian Theology, London, 1880.

Rattenbury, J.E. The Evangelical Doctrines of Charles Wesley's Hymns, London, 1942.

Rolle, R. The Fire of Love.

Sangster, W.E. The Path to Perfection, Epworth, 1957.

Schmidt, M. John Wesley (Two Volumes).

Southey, R. The Life of Wesley, London, 1846.

St. Bernard. On the Love of God.

St. John of the Cross. Vols 1-3 Ed. A. Pears, 1943.

Starkey, L.M. The Work of the Holy Spirit.

Taylor, J. Rules and Exercises of Holy living and Holy dying.

The Book of Common Prayer, London, 1851.

Wendel, F. Calvin. Fontana, 1972.

Willey, B.   The Eighteenth Century Background.   Chatto & Windus, 1940.

Williams, C.S.   John Wesley's Theology today.

Workman, H.B.   A new history of Methodism.

Wyon, O.   Desire for God.   Fontana, 1963.

St Paul's Cathedral

A SERVICE

IN THE PRESENCE OF
Her Majesty The Queen
AND
*His Royal Highness
The Duke Of Edinburgh*

TO CELEBRATE THE
*250th Anniversary
of the Conversion of
The Reverend John Wesley*

Tuesday 24th May 1988

4.30 pm

The Methodist Church

MAY 24th 1988
– THE 250TH ANNIVERSARY DAY
OF JOHN WESLEY'S CONVERSION

FRIEND, VISITOR, PILGRIM, welcome to this 250th Anniversary Celebration of the Conversion of John Wesley, "About a Quarter before nine" on Wednesday, May 24, 1738. Welcome to the London of Aldersgate and Little Britain and great St. Paul's. In the months of 1738 and 1739 John Wesley was himself a visitor here. Today the People called Methodists and their friends have come from all over the world to Wesley's London. Today, as we celebrate here – from Estonia in the north to Chile in the south and around the world in all the continents, thirty four millions in the United States amongst them – fifty four millions in ninety countries celebrate with us. And with the People called Methodists are our friends of the great communions of the Christian world, many acknowledging special debts to Wesley's vision; and, growing together, our emphases and our traditions become blended in a greater unity, to serve a still needful world.

IN 1738 Wesley, back from the Americas, Fellow of Lincoln College, Oxford, largely unknown, came here to London. In spiritual uncertainty he was feeling his way. The teacher, preacher, poet, organiser, traveller, publisher, inventor, builder, curer, carer, campaigner and reformer, the five foot and a bit high giant of the next half century seeking purpose for his life, felt compelled to be here. Here he talked, prayed and sang with the Moravian Christians, their English disciples, his own brother Charles, John Bray, and their friends. For a few months in a long life this square mile witnessed the spiritual birth of Methodism and the development of its missionary purpose, drawing on the Moravian inspiration but progressing to a vision of a world that might be looked upon as a parish filled with opportunities to proclaim the glad tidings of salvation.

IN this locality John Wesley came to his all enveloping conviction that through the full free grace of God alone, by faith, all may be saved and all may know that they are saved. Here at that same time, particularly following his German visit, the word "singing" starts to appear daily, and indeed several times a day, in his diary and Methodism became "born in song".

GREAT St. Paul's stood then, stands now. In Wesley's schooldays it was barely finished; today miraculously saved and constantly maintained it is the motherchurch of London. Then, a symbol of rebirth after the Great Fire, now it is a continuing symbol of faith in the City. This year we come together to St. Paul's not only because this is a great House of God, but because here John Wesley himself came to Evensong on his own conversion day. And, here, on the two days that followed he came again, and then again, seeking confirmation of his Aldersgate experience.

FRIEND, visitor and pilgrim, today is a day of Celebration for the whole Christian Church. Those who gather in St. Paul's and those who lead the worship are a sufficient witness to that truth. The People called Methodists and their friends give thanks to God! In thousands of services throughout the world, people have gathered to give thanks.

TODAY is about John Wesley's experience of the Spirit, at Aldersgate, in the City of London, two hundred and fifty years ago. Today is about God, about the continuing possibility of the experience of the Spirit, by Grace, through Faith, for all people.

FRIEND, VISITOR, PILGRIM! Welcome in the name of the Father, and of the Son, and the Holy Spirit, to great St. Paul's, in John Wesley's London.

(Continued on inside back cover)

From 3.45 pm: Music by the Trinity College of Music Chamber Orchestra

SAMUEL WESLEY

Symphony in D

GEORGE FRIDERIC HANDEL

Concerto Grosso in Bb major Op. 3 No. 2

ANTONIO VIVALDI

Concerto for 2 Trumpets in C

From 4.14 pm:

Organ Music

Prelude and Fugue in A minor   – Charles Wesley (1757 – 1834)

An Old English Melody   – Samuel Wesley (1766 – 1837)

March in D   – Samuel Wesley (1766 – 1837)

The Congregation remain seated until the fanfare sounds.

At 4.05 pm the Charles Wesley Hymn Choir take their places in the North Transept.

At 4.15 pm the Dean and Chapter together with the Bishop of London, the Archbishop of Canterbury and the President of the British Methodist Conference leave the Dean's Aisle and proceed to the West Door of the Cathedral.

At 4.17 pm the University of Birmingham Chaplaincy Choir, the College of Minor Canons, the Prebendaries and the Preacher proceed to their places in the Quire.

The Secretary of the British Methodist Conference, the Vice President of the British Methodist Conference, the representative of the Moderator of the Free Church Federal Council, the Primus of the Scottish Episcopal Church, a Bishop of the Moravian Church, the Cardinal Archbishop of Westminster, the past Moderator of the Church of Scotland and the presiding Bishop of the Methodist Church in Kenya proceed to their places under the Dome.

At 4.20 pm the Lord Mayor locum tenens arrives at the Cathedral and is received at the West Door by the Dean and Chapter together with the Bishop of London.

At 4.25 pm Her Majesty The Queen and His Royal Highness The Prince Philip, Duke of Edinburgh arrive at the Cathedral.

Her Majesty The Queen and His Royal Highness The Prince Philip, Duke of Edinburgh are received at the foot of the steps by the Lord Mayor locum tenens.

A fanfare is sounded and all stand.

Her Majesty The Queen and His Royal Highness are received at the West Door by the Dean and Chapter together with the Bishop of London, the Archbishop of Canterbury and the President of the British Methodist Conference.

ORDER OF PROCESSION

A Virger

The Aldersgate Cross

The President of the British Methodist Conference

The Archbishop's Secretary for Ecumenical Affairs

The Archbishop of Canterbury

The Dean's Virger

The Sacrist

The Dean and Chapter with the Bishop of London

His Royal Highness The Duke of Edinburgh	Her Majesty The Queen
	Lady in Waiting
Equerry	Private Secretary

ORDER OF SERVICE

THE PROCESSIONAL HYMN

'Hymn for the Anniversary Day of One's Conversion'

O for a thousand tongues to sing
My great Redeemer's praise,
The glories of my God and King,
The triumphs of his grace!

My gracious Master and my God,
Assist me to proclaim,
To spread through all the earth abroad
The honours of thy name.

Jesus — the name that charms our fears,
That bids our sorrows cease;
'Tis music in the sinner's ears,
'Tis life, and health, and peace.

He speaks; and, listening to his voice,
New life the dead receive;
The mournful, broken hearts rejoice;
The humble poor believe.

Choir
Only
See all your sins on Jesus laid:
The Lamb of God was slain;
His soul was once an offering made
For every soul of man.

In Christ, our Head, you then shall know,
Shall feel, your sins forgiven,
Anticipate your heaven below,
And own that love is heaven.

Words: Charles Wesley

Music: Thomas Phillips
Lydia

The Dean welcomes the Congregation.

God save our gracious Queen
Long live our noble Queen,
  God save the Queen:
Send her victorious,
Happy and glorious,
Long to reign over us:
  God save the Queen.

Thy choicest gifts in store
On her be pleased to pour;
  Long may she reign:
May she defend our laws,
And ever give us cause
To sing with heart and voice,
  God save the Queen.

Arranged by Gordon Jacob

All kneel or sit.

These Prayers, although abbreviated, are taken from the Methodist Covenant Service. John Wesley's first Covenant Service was held in the French Church at Spitalfields on the 11th August 1755. Although the words have been revised, the Covenant Service retains a special significance for the people called Methodists.

THE PRAYER OF ADORATION
led by
The President of the British Methodist Conference
The Reverend Dr William R Davies

Let us pray.

Let us adore the God of Love
who created us;
who continually preserves and sustains us.

**You are God; we praise you; we acknowledge you
to be the Lord.**

Let us glory in the grace of our Lord Jesus
Christ.
Though he was rich, yet for our sakes he became
poor;
who became obedient to death, death on the cross;
who was dead and is alive for ever;

You, Christ, are the King of Glory.

Let us rejoice in the fellowship of the Holy Spirit,
the Lord, the Giver of life,
whose witness confirms us;
whose wisdom teaches us;
whose power enables us.

All praise to you, Holy Spirit.

6

THE CONFESSION OF SIN

Let us humbly confess our sins to God.

Lord God, we confess with shame our slowness to
learn of your Son, our failure to follow him, our
reluctance to bear the cross.

We confess the poverty of our worship, our
evasion of responsibilities in your service, our
imperfect stewardship of your gifts.

Have mercy on us, Lord, and forgive us.

Let each of us in silence make our own confession to God.

SILENCE

**Have mercy on us, O God, according to your
steadfast love. Create in us a clean heart,
O God, and put a new and right spirit within us.**

If we confess our sins, he is faithful and just,
and will forgive our sins and cleanse us from all
unrighteousness.

Amen. Thanks be to God.

A READING FROM JOHN WESLEY'S JOURNAL
by
the Vice-President of the British Methodist Conference
Mr Derek Burrell

Wednesday, 24th May 1738

I think it was about five this Morning, that I opened my Testament on those Words. *There are given unto us exceeding great and precious Promises, even that ye should be Partakers of the divine Nature. 2 Pet. i.4.*

Just as I went out, I open'd it again on those Words, *Thou art not far from the Kingdom of God.*

In the Afternoon I was ask'd to go to *St. Paul's.* The Anthem was, *Out of the Deep have I call'd unto thee, O Lord: Lord, hear my Voice.*

Then the Charles Wesley Hymn Choir sings the Chorale:

> Aus tiefer Not schrei' ich zu dir,
>> Herr Gott, erhör' mein Rufen!
> Dein gnädig Ohren kehr' zu mir,
>> Und meiner Bitt' sie offen!
> Denn so du willt das sehen an,
>> Was Sünd' und Unrecht ist gethan,
> Wer kann, Herr, vor dir bleiben?
>
> Out of the deep I cry to thee;
>> Lord God, mark my contrition!
> Thy gracious ear incline to me,
>> And hear now my petition!
> If thou remembrest each misdeed,
>> If each should have its rightful meed,
> Who may abide thy presence?

Martin Luther 1524   *Johann Walther's Gesangbuch 1524*
Tr. Composite   Harmonised: by J S Bach

The Reading from the Journal continues:

In the Evening I went very unwillingly to a Society in *Aldersgate Street,* where one was reading *Luther's* Preface to the Epistle to the *Romans.* About a Quarter before nine, while he was describing the Change which God works in the Heart through Faith in *Christ,* I felt my Heart strangely warm'd. I felt I did trust in *Christ, Christ* alone for Salvation: And an Assurance was given to me, That He had taken away *my* Sins, even *mine*, and saved *me* from the Law of Sin and Death.

HYMN

O thou who camest from above
The pure celestial fire to impart,
Kindle a flame of sacred love
On the mean altar of my heart!

Then a large flame is lit by two children of the United Methodist Church of America.

Whilst the flame is being lit, Bishop Lawi Imathiu, Presiding Bishop of the Methodist Church in Kenya, Chairperson of the Executive Committee of the World Methodist Council, says:

We light this flame, that a flame of sacred love may be kindled in our hearts as it was in the hearts of John and Charles Wesley.

The hymn then continues:

There let it for thy glory burn
With inextinguishable blaze,
And trembling to its source return,
In humble prayer and fervent praise.

Jesus, confirm my heart's desire
To work, and speak, and think for thee;
Still let me guard the holy fire,
And still stir up thy gift in me—

Unison
Ready for all thy perfect will,
My acts of faith and love repeat,
Till death thy endless mercies seal,
And make the sacrifice complete.

Words: Charles Wesley

Music: S S Wesley
Hereford

Then all sit for: **THE EPISTLE**
Romans 5:1-5
read by
Mrs Georgette de Marke
of the Methodist Church in Sierra Leone

Therefore, since we are justified by faith, we have peace with God through our Lord Jesus Christ. Through him we have obtained access to this grace in which we stand, and we rejoice in our hope of sharing the glory of God. More than that, we rejoice in our sufferings, knowing that suffering produces endurance, and endurance produces character, and character produces hope, and hope does not disappoint us, because God's love has been poured into our hearts through the Holy Spirit which has been given to us.

This is the word of the Lord.

Thanks be to God.

All remain seated while the University of Birmingham Chaplaincy Choir sings:

"Come, let us preach the gospel"
South African Song

THE GOSPEL
John 15:1-4
read by
Mrs Sathiawathy J Anandanayagam
Vice-President of the Sri Lankan Methodist Conference

Jesus said,
I am the true vine, and my Father is the vinedresser. Every branch of mine that bears no fruit, he takes away, and every branch that does bear fruit he prunes, that it may bear more fruit. You are already made clean by the word which I have spoken to you. Abide in me, and I in you. As the branch cannot bear fruit by itself, unless it abides in the vine, neither can you, unless you abide in me.

This is the gospel of Christ.

Praise to Christ our Lord.

Then the organ shall play.

THE SERMON
by
The Reverend Dr Donald English
President of the Methodist Conference 1978,
Vice-Chairperson, The Executive Committee
of the World Methodist Council.

HYMN

Captain of Israel's host, and Guide
Of all who seek the land above,
Beneath thy shadow we abide,
   The cloud of thy protecting love;
Our strength, thy grace; our rule, thy word;
   Our end, the glory of the Lord.

By thine unerring Spirit led,
   We shall not in the desert stray;
We shall not full direction need,
   Nor miss our providential way;
As far from danger as from fear,
   While love, almighty love, is near.

Words: Charles Wesley   Music: Thomas Phillips
                                              Marienlyst

All kneel or sit.

THE PRAYER OF THANKSGIVING
led by
His Excellency, Sir Edney Cain,
The High Commissioner for Belize

All powerful and everliving God, we give you thanks and praise for the world you created and for your forgiving mercy shown to us in Jesus Christ. We thank you that for us he died on the cross, rose from the dead and ascended into heaven. We thank you for the Holy Spirit bearing witness with our spirits that we are your children.

We praise you that through your saints you have guided the Church in every age and that you gave to your servants John and Charles Wesley the assurance that you had taken away their sins. We glorify you that through them you raised up a people who have carried the flame of your love through many lands.

Pour out, we pray, your life-giving Spirit on us and all who bear the name of Christ that by faithful witness and service we may serve the present age and with all who have gone before come at last to heaven.

We ask this through Jesus Christ our Lord.

Amen.

THE PRAYERS OF INTERCESSION

The University of Birmingham Chaplaincy Choir sing the Alleluias.

Alleluia

The Canon in Residence says:

God, holy and loving, we pray for the Universal Church and on this day especially for the people called Methodists that together we may with one voice glorify you through Jesus Christ our Saviour.

Alleluia

The Bishop of the Moravian Church says:

We pray that by our words and by our lives we may show forth the good news, that many may be brought to accept your great and precious promises and become partakers of your divine nature.

Alleluia.

The Archbishop of Canterbury says:

We pray for Elizabeth our Queen and all her family, for all who lead the nations and for all people in their several callings, that they may so obey your royal law that the kingdoms of this world may become the kingdom of Christ.

Alleluia.

The Cardinal Archbishop of Westminster says:

We pray for the poor, the oppressed, the powerless, the prisoners of conscience, the hostages, the sick and the suffering, that they may have courage and hope.

Alleluia.

Hear our prayers, we ask, not for our merits but for the sake of Jesus Christ, your Son our Lord.

Amen.

THE PRAYER OF DEDICATION

Led by the President of the British Methodist Conference, all say:

Almighty God we offer you through Christ
our souls and bodies to be a living sacrifice:
send us out in the power of your Spirit
to spread scriptural holiness throughout the world.
Amen.

The President says:

As Christ has taught us, we are bold to say:

THE LORD'S PRAYER

Our Father, who art in heaven,
hallowed be thy name;
thy kingdom come;
thy will be done;
on earth as it is in heaven.
Give us this day our daily bread.
And forgive us our trespasses,
as we forgive those who trespass against us.
And lead us not into temption;
but deliver us from evil.
For thine is the kingdom, the power, and the glory,
for ever and ever.
Amen.

All stand to sing the hymn, during which flames are lit from the main flame and dispersed to various areas of the Cathedral, as a token of our commitment to live the life of Christ in the world.

HYMN

Love divine, all loves excelling,
   Joy of heaven to earth come down,
Fix in us thy humble dwelling,
   All thy faithful mercies crown.
Jesu, thou art all compassion,
   Pure, unbounded love thou art;
Visit us with thy salvation,
   Enter every trembling heart.

Come, almighty to deliver,
   Let us all thy life receive;
Suddenly return, and never,
   Never more thy temples leave.
Thee we would be always blessing,
   Serve thee as thy hosts above,
Pray, and praise thee, without ceasing,
   Glory in thy perfect love.

Unison

Finish then thy new creation,
   Pure and spotless let us be;
Let us see thy great salvation,
   Perfectly restored in thee:
Changed from glory into glory,
   Till in heaven we take our place,
Till we cast our crowns before thee,
   Lost in wonder, love, and praise!

Words: Charles Wesley

Music: W.P. Rowlands
Blaenwern

THE BLESSING
by
The Bishop of London

The peace of God, which passes all understanding, keep your hearts and minds in the knowledge and love of God, and of his Son Jesus Christ our Lord: and the blessing of God Almighty, the Father, the Son and the Holy Spirit, be amongst you and remain with you always.

Amen.

THE DISMISSAL
by
The President of the British Methodist Conference

Go forth in Christ's name;
Make his will your resolve;
Find his presence in all you do,
And serve him with joy
Till he comes in glory.

Amen.

The Service ended, the Dean and Chapter, together with the Bishop of London, the Archbishop of Canterbury, the President of the British Methodist Conference and the Preacher conduct Her Majesty The Queen to the West Door.

The Secretary of the British Methodist Conference, the Vice-President of the British Methodist Conference, and the presiding Bishop of the Methodist Church in Kenya proceed to the West Door to be presented to Her Majesty the Queen.

The Lord Mayor locum tenens proceeds to the West Door.

The College of Minor Canons, the Prebendaries, the representative of the Moderator of the Free Church Federal Council, the Primus of the Scottish Episcopal Church, a Bishop of the Moravian Church, the Cardinal Archbishop of Westminster and the past Moderator of the Church of Scotland return to the Dean's Aisle.

Organ Postlude: *Choral Song.*   Samuel Sebastian Wesley.

Music by the Trinity College of Music Chamber Orchestra.
Suite No. 1 in F from the Water Music.   George Frideric Handel.

Members of the Congregation are asked to remain in their places until it
is indicated by the ushers that they are free to leave.

The bells of the Cathedral will be rung by members of the Guild of
Ringers of St. Paul's Cathedral.

Organist: Dr Christopher Dearnley

Trinity College of Music Chamber Orchestra and Descant Trumpeters
Conductor: David Pettit

Trumpeters of the Life Guards
by permission of
Colonel A.H. Parker- Bowles OBE
(Lieutenant-Colonel Commanding Household Cavalry)

University of Birmingham Chaplaincy Choir

The Charles Wesley Hymn Choir

Director of Music: G. Victor Henry

The Methodist Church wishes to express its thanks to the Dean and
Chapter of St. Paul's Cathedral for their co-operation in the preparation
of the service.

THE SERVICE

This service celebrates the Conversion of John Wesley at Aldersgate following his visit to Evensong at St. Paul's Cathedral on May 24th 1738. It recalls that historic day, celebrates Methodism's spread to many countries throughout the world and reminds us that we are called to "spread sacred love".

The structure of the service is based upon the Methodist Sunday Service – the Preparation, the Ministry of the Word and the Response.

Hymns play an important part in worship and Methodists are known as people who sing their theology. The hymns by Charles Wesley, converted a few days before his brother John, are used. "O for a Thousand tongues to sing", like many of Wesley's hymns, shows his remarkable ability to quote or interpret scripture. "O thou who camest from above", has the image of fire which can be traced back to Leviticus 6 v 13 and is used by many spiritual writers such as St. John of the Cross. "Captain of Israel's host and Guide" traditionally ends the Annual Conference of British Methodism; it reminds us of our spiritual journey, and echoes Exodus 13 where God's People were led through the desert by a pillar of cloud. Wesley's triumphant hymn, "Love divine", expresses God's great love to us through Christ, with Wesley taking us in the final verse from time to eternity.

The **reading** from the Epistle to the Romans highlights a main feature of John Wesley's preaching, that of Justification by Faith, whilst the Gospel reminds us of our call to be one with Christ. The events of the 24th May 1738 are recounted from Wesley's Journal, with the Anthem dividing the afternoon and evening events.

The trinitarian **Prayers** of Adoration and Confession although adapted, are from "A service for such as would make or renew their Covenant with God". The Covenant Service is used in Methodist Churches at the begining of each year. Later this evening the Celebration at Aldersgate Street will conclude with the Covenant itself. "Alleluia", from the Taizé Community in France, is used in the Prayers of Intercession.

Happily the participation of people from various parts of the world reflects the spread of the Methodist movement, whilst the song, "O Come let us preach the Gospel" is written by Christians from South Africa.

After the first verse of the hymn "O thou who camest from above" a large flame is lit under the Dome, symbolic of sacred love; later during the final hymn a liturgical movement takes place and candles lit from the central flame are carried to all parts of the Cathedral. These candles come from the Church of the Holy Sepulchre in Jerusalem and are similar to those used in the Orthodox service of the "Giving of the light" on Easter Eve. The dispersal of the light remind us of our commitment to spread sacred love in our world.

The Methodist Church is part of the "Holy Catholic Church" and it is with especial joy that we welcome representative Church Leaders as participants in this service.

In humility we offer to God this celebration of worship. Let it be to his praise and glory.